WE CAN

WE CAN DRIVE THERE

Juliet Greenwood

First published in Great Britain in 2023 by
The Book Guild Ltd
Unit E2 Airfield Business Park,
Harrison Road, Market Harborough,
Leicestershire. LE16 7UL
Tel: 0116 2792299
www.bookguild.co.uk
Email: info@bookguild.co.uk
Twitter: @bookguild

Copyright © 2023 Juliet Greenwood

The right of Juliet Greenwood to be identified as the author of this
work has been asserted by them in accordance with the
Copyright, Design and Patents Act 1988.

All rights reserved. No part of this publication may be
reproduced, transmitted, or stored in a retrieval system, in any form or by any means,
without permission in writing from the publisher, nor be otherwise circulated in
any form of binding or cover other than that in which it is published and without
a similar condition being imposed on the subsequent purchaser.

Typeset in 11pt Minion Pro

Printed and bound by CPI Group (UK) Ltd, Croydon, CR0 4YY

ISBN 978 1915352 576

British Library Cataloguing in Publication Data.
A catalogue record for this book is available from the British Library.

For William – I might dream it but you make it happen.

Prologue

"We can drive there!"

Those words heralded the beginning of our love affair with road tripping to Hungary. Right after I had also just said, "Where the **** is Hungary?", and I am not a person given to swearing but this seemed to warrant it. Because back then, in 2005 when I made that dramatic proclamation (albeit, to myself at first), we, genuinely, were not entirely sure where Hungary was. That opening line was based on a quick look at an actual map (a folded-out paper map no less) and then I sent it as a text to my husband Will's Blackberry. From there, the road trip baby began to form, and a birth plan was drawn up.

Looking at that map that day did two things. Firstly, it opened up the world of possibilities that had started the day we bought a 'really big car' back in 2002. In effect, thanks to that action, we had given ourselves the 'wings', not that we needed a plane, because, as I said at the beginning, I could see quite clearly, by looking at my actual paper map, that we could drive there. Secondly, it highlighted the massive black hole in our education. Despite being reasonably intelligent people, both with degrees, and Will a teacher, it was pretty clear our geography sucked. How could we have no idea where Hungary was? I studied European History for A-level a million years ago and there was definitely talk about the Austro-Hungarian Empire. But had we never studied a map? And why, the moment I try to remember anything from my history studies that might be at all useful, did the name Talleyrand pop into my head? Who was Talleyrand? A quick Google search reveals that he was French and around at the time of the French Revolution. So, neither Austrian nor Hungarian, but I bet he knew where both countries were! And now so did I. I could even see a clear route to get there. We could drive anywhere we bloody well wanted. Like, everywhere is in walking distance, if you have the time. We didn't need a plane. We had wheels.

First stop would be France (where Talleyrand lived) after a quick tunnel across the Channel. France is big, but we would only need to go through the top corner to get into Belgium, and how bad could driving through Belgium be? Sweet little place, home to some of our favourite things – chocolate, Tintin, Eddy Merckx – and next to our favourite country, the Netherlands. Then into Germany and all the way across it in a straight line. Wow, Germany is big too! Huge. Enormous. No speed limit though, anyone who has watched *Top Gear* knows that. We can just whizz across superfast, no problem. I am sure that will work, in an old, rusty bus. Aah yes, our 'really big car'. Now might be a good time to introduce you to the vehicle. I am not talking about just any old rusty bus but one of Germany's own, a 1986 Volkswagen T25, so it does not really 'whizz' anywhere, but at least if anything goes wrong in Germany, they will know how to fix it. In fact, it gives me great comfort to know that we will be travelling through the more Germanic countries of Europe. We will be safe there. They will recognise their prodigal... offspring?

We bought 'The Bus', as she was usually referred to back then, in 2002 when we had a fourth child. Fact: you cannot fit four kids in a normal-sized car (a five-seater), and if you buy a people carrier, a seven-seater, you will find that the extra row of seating is in the boot space. So where do you put all your stuff? Four kids require a lot of stuff. Plus, we are not really people carrier people (our 'normal-sized car' was a 2CV, so that explains a lot – admit it, three paragraphs in and you are already getting a picture), so we looked at the cooler campervans, the T2s, but most of them are more kitchen than seating and at that point we were needing something to just be our car. The idea of sleeping in it would come later.

We found a bus for sale in Hereford, brought over from South Africa when the family who owned her moved back here. They had loved her so much they could not bear to leave her behind but now their own hoard of kids had all grown up, so it was time for another family to love her. There was no kitchen, just two bench seats facing each other in the back and an enormous boot big enough for a ten-year-old to almost stand up straight in and do a few keepy-ups! Is it weird that I use that as a unit of measurement? I saw him do it and he had room!

'She' is a little more rectangular than the classic surfer campervan but still cool enough to get the recognition on the road. Not air-cooled but engine at the back, under the enormous boot space, where it should be. Yellow and white, she was beautiful, and it was love at first sight. Literally, as we turned into their driveway, and we saw her for the first time, parked there, waiting for us, I said, "Oh that looks like us." And that is a good a method as any to make a decision on buying a car. It looked like us. So, we added a few seatbelts to the back and for four years she was just a car, for the school run when we did not go by bike, for the shopping and for the hobbies, horses, football, cheerleading, theatre trips and visiting family. We first spread our 'wings' in 2004 and drove to Paris to show the kids that beautiful city. Driving around the Arc de Triomphe in daytime Parisian traffic is an experience you will never forget, or possibly survive, so we cheated and did it at night. It was still a thrill, almost as much as then driving back to our campsite through the Bois de Boulogne and seeing the interesting nightlife that goes on in the bushes there... while trying to explain it to the kids. We also went to Denmark, catching the ferry across from Harwich with Leo Sawyer (we are 99% certain it was him in the queue ahead of us), driving across the country from the port on the west coast to Copenhagen over on the east, crossing a bridge with such a huge toll on it that we are fairly sure we now own that bridge and having a wonderful time in the Tivoli gardens and exploring the city. If your kids like climbing towers, then this is the city for you.

Now I was looking at a map of Europe as if I had never seen one before and planning an actual road trip, driving across four countries, with four kids (in 2006 aged sixteen, twelve, nine and four) and sleeping where we parked each night. After the long trek across Germany, we would get to Austria, place of nuns, mountains, skiers, cakes and our friend Gwynn and his family (so one night of free accommodation – check). And then, remember that A-level History? Next to Austria is… Hungary. They used to be linked politically, but borders changed, there were wars, stuff happened and now they are separate countries. To be fair to us, and make an excuse for our stupidity, Hungary was hidden behind an iron curtain for most of our formative years, but unlike Poland which disappeared completely at one point in history, it has always been there. Next to Austria. Part of the one big landmass that is Europe, all joined together and connected by roads. As I said at the beginning, we could drive there. And so, a plan was formed – a quick dash across France and Belgium, speed across Germany, into Austria, say hallo to Gwynn and then we would be there: Hungary.

Since that first trip in 2006, when we realised we could drive to Hungary, we have done many more thousands of kilometres in 'The Bus'. We have followed the Tour de France three times, driven to Barcelona as well on one of those trips and visited Disneyland Paris on another. In 2010 we started going skiing at New Year, so 'The Bus' got us down to the Alps where we stayed near Lake Annecy and to the resort at La Clusaz every day in some interesting weather conditions. She has done that journey six more times and only missed two years when she was off the road having some extensive spa treatment from Ben. In 2015 she was reborn as Olive and, to celebrate, took us to Transylvania! We have also been to our other favourite country beginning with H, Holland, four or five times, visiting friends, buying Dutch bikes, combining the road trip with a cycle tour (we have been cycling in Holland every year for nearly thirty years now, which you can read about in my other book *It's Like Survivor!)* In 2016 Olive nearly outshone the bride at our eldest daughter's wedding, the sight of Maisie in her beautiful yellow dress matching Olive's new paintwork – her six pastel-clad bridesmaids all spilling out of the big side door of her 'wedding car' was just one of the gorgeous images from that wonderful day. We have given this bus a great life and she has returned the favour. There have been seven trips to Hungary. This story follows one of those journeys, in 2017, but has all the others mixed in and some more. Fasten your seatbelts, it is going to be bumpy, though we do try to avoid the potholes!

Why Hungary? That, dear reader, is a good question. And, luckily for you, it has a good answer which I will eventually get to. Settle in.

Firstly though, the disclaimer. This is *not* a guidebook. It is *not* a 'how to' book. It is probably wildly inaccurate about many, many things. Any historical or geographical facts have been Googled and just put in to make me look clever. I have put in roads taken and junctions missed, towns passed and supermarkets visited, so you might be able to follow our route if you really wanted to, but I sincerely doubt you will. This is also *not* a book for the purposes of education or enlightenment. It is for pure entertainment and, hopefully, that feeling you get when you watch people struggle to become olive farmers in the beautiful Tuscan hills. It seems a good idea, looks pretty, but you are glad that it is not you.

Too much like hard work. Much easier to be slumped on your sofa watching, with a glass of Italian wine in hand.

And the dedication: to all the people who have helped keep Olive on the road, our first mechanic Robin, the guys at Colwells in Gloucester and to Ben, our friend who just happens to be an excellent mechanic with the type of 'can-do' attitude we love. Well, he certainly did it, laboured over her to make her beautiful on the outside and run smoothly on the inside and is always on the end of the phone with his infinite mechanical wisdom and patient advice. And to Emma who did the important job of putting the decal on 'The Bus' to rename her Olive after hubby Ben's hard work in 2014. Thanks to Tim for inspiring her new name, texting me one day to tell me he had just watched *Little Miss Sunshine* and had thought of us. It's a T2 in the film but it is yellow, and they have to push it a lot. Very us. Talking of pushing, a massive debt of gratitude is owed to all those people who have helped us to start with a bump, friends and family but also the many kind strangers in petrol stations, lay-bys, car parks, campsites, on the road itself, I hope you will read this and remember. We do. None of this would have been possible without you. We would, quite literally, never have got anywhere.

Day One

In 2019, the last time we made this journey, before Covid-19 struck and we left Europe, we had run out of kids who wanted to sweat in the back of Olive for hours on end (kids are weird like that), so we just took the dog instead. Packing for him included a mountain of food, poo bags, a cooling bandana and mat, his own paddling pool, a tie-out stake, an endless supply of spherical objects to play with, a sleeping mat, towels and bowls. So, apart from the rabies shot, not that different to travelling with kids, and the dog never once asked if we were nearly there. He is in sync with Olive too. Will, my co-pilot on the road and in life, likes to stop every couple of hours to check on oil and water levels and let Olive have a rest. This gives the dog the perfect opportunity to stretch his legs and check his own liquid levels.

In 2017 however, when this story is set, we were travelling with the dog *and* fifteen-year-old Doris who was coming with us on this leg but then flying back with her older siblings from Budapest leaving us to return alone for the first time. As we drove off from our home in Gloucester, I called, "See you in Budapest," out of the window to second middle child, twenty-year-old Walter. I thought this sounded cool and James Bondish, but I am fairly sure it was greeted with an eye roll. Say 'see you in Budapest' with Sean Connery's accent and you will see what I mean. It *is* cool. Walt would meet us there in six days' time, with Maisie (our eldest) and her husband Adam, and Meredith, the first middle child. It is not rocket science that your grown-up kids will deign to holiday with you if you pay for most of it. But it is cool that they have their own money to occasionally pay for stuff too now. I guess we also quite like each other, but the real attraction for the kids is the return to Hungary. They all absolutely love it there. For reasons that will soon be revealed.

Apart from the dog's extensive luggage requirements, Olive was loaded up with clothes, books, food, cooking stuff, including a petrol stove, cups, plates and cutlery, of course a kettle, some pans, bedding, pillows, towels and toiletries, toilet rolls, wipes, first aid, hats, sunglasses, macs, sweets, more books, real maps, battery-powered lights, important car documents and passports. And tools, a jack, oil, water, coolant and never leave home without duct tape and wire. As The Rock says, 'if you can't fix it with duct tape, then you ain't using enough duct tape'. This theory goes for wire too where Olive is concerned. We also had a table and some chairs and a bowl that we use for a kitchen sink.

Who sits where was laid down by ordinance back in 2002 when baby Doris was in a car seat nearest the door and biggest sister Maisie sat next to her on the forward-facing of the two bench seats just in case she was needed to administer attention on her baby sister. Being the eldest she was considered the most responsible one for this job. Or

Day One

she drew the short straw, one or the other. Walt sits opposite Maisie, his back to the driver, as far away from Doris as possible, and Meredith sits behind me, in charge of opening the sliding door and where she can sit with her feet sticking out of the side windows to catch the breeze. I get shotgun, though always happy to swap with someone in the back as it is fun for them to ride up front in the huge cab area and chat to the driver, and I never mind a chance to stretch out more in the back and read or snooze. On this day though, in 2017, we set off with the dog in Walt's place, on a cushion, wearing a special harness attaching him to the seatbelt, his nose in easy reach of the side sliding window. Doris is still in her usual seat, no longer in a car seat but surrounded by pillows and blankets and, most often, from about two minutes into the journey, asleep. We have a photo of seven-year-old Doris in that very spot with a little sign in front of her saying 'wake me up when we get to Annecy' on a trip to watch the Tour de France time trial around the lake there. It can take us over eleven hours to get from Calais to Annecy. Doris was probably asleep for most of it!

When travelling a long distance in a thirty-five-year-old bus there are many hold-your-breath-and-hope moments. Not unlike Maisie when she was learning to drive, passing between two parked cars with a 'phew'. "What do you mean 'phew'?" asked her horrified dad.

"Well, I didn't know if we were going to make it." So, *stop*! The first of these 'phew we made it' moments invariably comes at customs. Firstly, I must say how much we absolutely love the tunnel – it is so perfect for travellers such as us who often have only the vaguest idea of how long a journey might take. If you do happen to miss your booked crossing it is no problem to get onto a later crossing, sometimes for free, sometimes for a small charge. You don't even need to know your pin number; it just sucks your card in and spits it back out. This came in handy in 2013 when we had some issues, to be detailed later, missed our crossing by more than twenty-four hours and had forgotten our credit card pin. On a good day it takes us about four hours to get there from Gloucester, though once we were leaking something from the moment we set off so had to return home, get it fixed first thing the next day by our amazing local garage and then try again after twenty-four hours had elapsed from our original crossing time. We have also been delayed by the buzzer (more of that later) and one time, by an essential detour to the big garden centre at Burford to buy garden wire (*never* travel without some). So, it is a four-hour journey on an excellent day. Once we have arrived, there are certain elements that do not vary. For one, it is particularly enjoyable to sit in the ticket queue and know that everyone else in the queue has clocked you. Some look with envy, many with derision, most with respect, but they all look. Secondly, the officials and staff are always very friendly and often make remarks such as 'it's nice to see something different' and 'are you sure you'll make it?' when we tell them where we are going. We always appreciate a joke about Olive, more so if it is made by someone packing heat, such as at customs. We have been stopped a couple of times and they pull you over and swab the steering wheel and door handles. We have no idea what it is they are looking for. If it is drugs, then surely the long-haired beardy guy driving the flowery campervan is a bit too obvious? And yes, that is an accurate description of my husband, Will, the driver. Though Olive lost her flowers after the 2014 refurb.

Once through customs and passport control, we need to go past the person who asks if we have LPG on board. They assume we have a cooker, but we have a stove powered in the same fashion as Olive, with petrol and crossed fingers. Then we join the high vehicle queue, although at 1.85 metres we only just qualify. It does cost a little more, but it is nice being in the double height compartment on the train with the coaches and other campervans. Not that claustrophobia is an issue for any of us; we do not even think about hurtling through the mud many metres under a large body of water. This time our booked train was at 10.50am but we have been put on the 11.20am which leaves at 11.05am. This fluidity of motion is what makes the tunnel so great and once that train starts to move it is only thirty-five minutes before you are on French soil. Park close to the car in front, windows open, handbrake on, we know the drill. We never use the toilets unless necessary – although the signs tell you where the toilets are, they don't tell you if you are closer to the front or the back so which are the best ones to go for. Will does break the rule of not walking between vehicles to get out and put tape on the headlights to reflect the glare the other way for continental driving. Then it is just time to have a little snooze, read a few pages of your book or have some last-minute concerns, like, should the dog have tags that make it clear he is English? Mental note to get +44 put on the next ones. And teach the dog to bark 'I'm lost' in French/German/Italian etc.

France

The train comes above ground and daylight, not fish, can be seen through the windows. Then it is a nervous wait to be directed off. Nervous because there was one time (one time?) when Olive was being very reluctant to start, and I had to push her off the train, much to the bemusement of the people in the car behind. She usually bump-starts well, even on the flat, so it is not a problem, it is just preferable if she starts on the key. This time though, she roars into life, and we drive off with a cheery wave to the train people. Up and onto the slip road, it is one way so 'side of the road' is not an issue. Our first stop in France is literally two hundred metres from the train. There is a petrol station on this exit road, and we always stop here for the toilets, for petrol, for one-euro coffee that tastes great because it is French, for liquid checks and for the dog. Across the way you can see the cars queuing to return to England, and from our grand position of 'just arrived', we feel sorry for them. Their adventure is over; ours is just beginning. When we leave that petrol station our holiday begins. Will immediately adapts to driving on the 'wrong' side of the road by trying to turn left when I tell him to take a right. He is scarily good at going round roundabouts the 'wrong' way and it only takes a few miles of looking over the wrong shoulder for him to get back into the groove. In a hire car at least, you can see what is coming up behind you in your blind spot even if you do keep punching the door to change gear. In your own right-hand side car, there is nothing quite like the adrenalin rush of trying to pull out into fast-moving traffic when you are essentially sitting on the wrong side of the car.

You must really, really trust your left-side sitting passengers to put their heads out and shout '*go now*' at the appropriate moment.

We have only been on the continent for twenty minutes and we have noticed a police car behind us and, without wanting to sound paranoid: We. Have. Noticed. A. Police. Car. Behind. Us. That does sound paranoid, doesn't it? Well, let us see if we can work out why. Time for some maths. Between 2006 and 2017 we have made this journey five times, so that is ten journeys in total, across and back, passing through five countries, clocking up approximately twenty-five thousand kilometres, and in that time, on all those journeys we have had seven police interactions, four in Germany, one in France, Belgium and Hungary each and none in Austria. Now, if my maths is correct, seven out of ten is greater than a 50% chance of being stopped. So, I think I am allowed to sound paranoid. The one time we were stopped in France it was the customs police and they made us follow them off the motorway to the services and then they asked us if we were carrying more than ten thousand euros. Even they could barely keep a straight face as they asked such a ridiculous question, and obviously, we answered no, so they were soon complimenting Olive and joking with Will, in French, about her. It was all very jolly, and we were able to continue our journey with the minimum of interruption, interrogation or intrusive searches. The incident in Belgium was even more minor – we had pulled ourselves up for petrol and a police officer came onto the forecourt and peered into the windows at the children lolling around in the back. "Seatbelts?" he asked, as it was obvious at least one of them, Walt lying full length on one seat, was not wearing one. I explained that we had taken them off to get out to go to the toilets and he seemed happy with that and wandered off.

This time the police car overtakes us and drives past with barely a side glance. Wait until we get to Germany though. That is where the cat and mouse game we play with the police will begin in earnest. Today though we are left in peace to play the 'What's That Noise?' game. This year we have some new sounds to interpret as we roll along, a slight clunk coming from the left front undercarriage that is worse over bumps; it might even be coming from the left front wheel accompanied by a metallic swishing sound that we have heard before and ended up being a wheel bearings issue. I like to ignore these noises; Will takes the opposite approach and likes to dwell on them at length. I am the yin to his yang and it is why we make such a great team. There is one noise that is missing this year though, and that is the sound of a buzzer going off. Incessantly. It was supposed to be an oil warning alarm, but it soon became a 'you are driving' alert and was on *all* the time. It became the mechanical equivalent of crying wolf. In the early days Will used to stop as soon as it went off as it tells you to do in the manual, but after a while, we would literally drive for hours with the blasted thing droning in our ears. It had two tones, one bearable, one not so, but both ignorable. Oil was checked regularly; it really was not warning us at all. If you Google 'oil warning buzzer' you can join a multitude of forums where other VW T25 owners are lamenting the same issue. So eventually we decided to do something drastic. Will, with our friend Tim for moral support, and the aid of a YouTube video, found the correct bit of circuit board in the dashboard, bent down the contact and silenced it forever.

There will always be mechanicals; this story will be littered with them. It is the price you pay for character. Some are quite minor, like the time the sliding door would not open easily so we had to climb in and out through the boot. Although, the reason the door would not open was because an essential bolt had been sequestered to fix a much bigger problem, more of that later. Some issues are born out of a moment of stupidity like leaving the oil cap on the roadside after an oil check and only realising at the time of the next oil check. Top tip – a medium-sized Nescafe jar lid is the perfect size to replace it with. Of course, it is the wrong thread so Will fashioned a wire cage, like on a champagne cork, to hold it in place. One year, in the whole of the 4,500-kilometre round trip, the only mishap was a lost windscreen wiper. We had come off the tunnel, made our petrol stop and just got out onto the Calais ring road when the wiper blade fell off. It was not even raining! Will had nudged the stalk by accident which turned on the wipers – they did two sweeps of the windscreen and then, thunk, one just fell off. Passenger side so we did not make too big a deal of it. I don't need to see where we are going, although I am the one reading the map. We were to lose one in 2019, again, on the passenger side, so we just drive through the rain with the one.

Oh yes, we are doing it old school, following signs and using a map. We need to head up towards Dunkirk then towards Lille and hopefully find a supermarket on the way, to buy some lunch provisions. It is thirty-two degrees; there is a long tailback on the other side of the road; and because it is hot, we have the windows open. As usual, we are the only car on the road that does. We do not have air conditioning, just windows that wind down, or slide. The curtains are flapping merrily in the breeze and the dog is sleeping peacefully on his cushion beneath them. Outside, the countryside is typical Northern France, flat farmland, industrial pockets, not particularly pretty. By 2017 we know this road well; it has been the starting point for so many trips. We know which exit takes you to McDonald's (forty-four), or for shopping in Decathlon (forty-three), for Calais town centre (forty-three) where there is also a campsite and for the Tunnel sous la Manche (forty-two). There are also brown information signs which we have seen many times yet not always been able to work out what they mean. As information signs go, they are not highly informative. Some depict occupations, presumably local to that area; others are obviously historical events like the one that translates as 'field of the cloth of gold' and refers to the meeting of Henry VIII and the King of France, Francois I on the 7th of June (my birthday!) 1520 (not my birthday!) in such a magnificent manner that the site of the festival was referred to as the field of the cloth of gold because of the expense of the event. Another sign just says 'Gravelines', and I have no idea what that refers to, so I have to Google it. It is a town and the site of a battle fought during the twelve-year war between France and Spain (1547–1559) on the 13th of July (our wedding anniversary) 1558 (feels like we have been married that long sometimes!). The town is twinned with Dartford in the UK, which is close to where my family are from, and Faskrudsbordur in Iceland, if anyone is from there?

We are on the A16/E40 and Lille is still eighty-nine kilometres away. France is a big place, and we were hoping to get into Germany tonight. Our comfortable cruising speed is eighty-eight kilometres per hour, so it takes us a while to get anywhere. The next sign says seventy-nine kilometres. That is the great thing about kilometres: they go down a lot faster than miles, so you do feel like you are getting somewhere faster. As Olive is from South Africa her speedo is in kmph, so we do not even have to convert. We could cut the corner off by heading towards Luxembourg, but we tried that one year and it did not end well. We stopped for some food, ordered some burgers and were dismayed to have them served to us as a plain burger in... a paper bag! No bun, no sauce, not even the gherkin that no one wants, just a dry burger in a paper bag. So, we have held that against Luxembourg ever since and refuse, absolutely refuse, to cross the border, not until they start importing some bread products.

While being distracted thinking about Luxembourg and naked burgers, talking about Bill Bryson and discussing the three Lamborghinis that had been at the tunnel in England, we nearly miss our turn off and must squeeze into a gap behind a hay lorry and cut across the hatchings. A25/E42 Lille sixty-five kilometres. It is a landscape of nations here as the cornfields and tractors look like England; the wide, flat vista is very Dutch; there are squat grey Norman churches and Spanish-style tall, tree-lined roads. We get a wave of acknowledgement from a VW on the other side of the road. We are accepted by the T2s as well as our own Transporter style if it is from the same era. There is a friendly camaraderie on the road if you are driving a vehicle of character, especially at services. People will pop over to chat. One time we met a man from Denmark, tall and blond, dressed all in black, driving a bulletproof car. Sounds like a country and western song. He was parked near to us at the services, so he pointed out his car. It was an ex-diplomat's car that he had bought in an auction in Copenhagen. He was on his way back to Denmark from Paris where he had been robbed at gunpoint a few days previously. It is a horrible thought being robbed at gunpoint, but you would think the guy in the bulletproof car would be the one who was immune from that fear. Trouble came when he rolled down the window and made his car as un-bulletproof as the rest of us. The robbery left him with no passport and no money, but his embassy had helped him out so he could at least return home. We had a chat; he admired our non-bulletproof bus; and we commiserated with him on his bad luck and wished him safe travels. The world is a scary place, and though we are under no illusion that driving across Europe is an adventure on the scale of climbing Everest or dodging drug lords in South America, as the man from Denmark in his bulletproof car showed us, trouble can find you on the streets of Paris if you ask directions from the wrong person as much as in the jungles of Bolivia.

We are nearly in Belgium, about as far from Bolivia as you could be! There will not be a magic moment as we cross the border; the landscape will continue from Northern France to Belgium without respite; it will still be flat and a little grey though the round rolls of hay soften the edges and there are shots of colour from orange tiled roofs. The only thing that will mark the change will be the number plates which will become the red Belgian ones rather than the yellow of France. Lille is now fifty-seven kilometres away; we are passing junction thirteen signposted Leper (Ypres), a name everyone knows but not all can pronounce (I think you say 'Eep'). One hundred years ago the medieval town of Ypres was reduced to rubble as the Battle of Passchendaele raged around it. You cannot forget the war around here, even if you are young enough to be untouched by it, there are physical reminders, the 'pillboxes' or lookouts in fields, bullet scars on cathedral walls and the place names, Verdun, Cambrai and the Somme.

History makes you hungry. It is lunchtime, so we duck off the motorway to find a town with a supermarket. Junction twelve serves us well with the town of Bailleul and an Aldi. It is a typical French town, tall cream-coloured houses with tiny windows and hanging baskets, painted shutters, grand municipal buildings and dominating churches. All very picturesque, but we choose to eat our lunch of bread, brie, ham and tomatoes in the Aldi car park. Off topic but here goes, European Aldi has a range of cat food called Juliet (the dog food is Romeo) and, thanks Aldi, also cat litter. My name can be spelled in a few different ways; usually over here it is with a double t and an e, but for the purposes of naming their pet products they have chosen to spell it how I spell it, the way Shakespeare spelled it, one e one t. I am not sure how I feel about that. It makes for a funny photo on Facebook though, and so I take a quick selfie with a tin of cat food.

We Can Drive There

The ever-present mechanical issues of Olive make a play for attention after lunch as a particularly sharp turn coming out of Aldi elicits a loud clanking from underneath. It is giving Will cause for concern and major stress, but he is taking the 'ignore it' approach and does not want to stop and have a look at what it might be. Sometimes this strategy can be remarkably effective. Other times... I keep quiet on this one and so on we clank. Lille is thirty-one kilometres, then we aim for Charleroi and Namur and on to Huy. This last town has been our favoured first night destination for many years now since we discovered a parking area which is okay for overnight sleeping. Huy is a big town with a huge river running through it. We sleep next to this river and across it is a supermarket and shopping centre with toilets. High above us is a castle with some sort of a cable car system to access it. Some years ago, we were watching *The Missing* and recognised the castle and the hotel under it and then the exact spot where we have cleaned our teeth. This trip though, because we set off a lot earlier than usual, we are travelling with the intention of bypassing the Huy stop and getting into Germany instead. We need to do two more hours of driving to make this happen. On our right some deer are peacefully grazing in a field; on our left a furious French trucker is beeping at us for not letting him in when he was overtaking us. It might have helped if he had indicated rather than relying on mind reading, but we have overtaken him back now (it must have been a downhill stretch), so that will learn him, as Will's grandad liked to say when teaching a valuable life lesson!

The dog is asleep, but Doris has now woken up from her post-lunch nap. We went a bit wrong after Lille (future ref –

must follow signs to Valenciennes) because I was distracted by Meredith phoning up to question me about Walter and their timings for when they fly out to meet us next week. I am not entirely sure what she expects me to do about it from two countries away because, yay, we finally crossed into Belgium while I was on the phone to her, but I could only reassure her that Walt is a very quick packer, so despite being at work on the day they are leaving, he will be ready in time (spoiler alert – he was). It is 4.00pm and we are in Belgium.

Belgium

Liege is on the boards – 167 kilometres or 105 miles. Tournai looks nice from the signs, huge cathedral with a rose window, the Grand Place, twelfth-century belfry, Romanesque church and medieval Red Fort tower. These information signs are full of information! If only we had time to stop but sadly, we can only enjoy the two thousand years of history that Tournai has to offer from its motorway sign. Apparently, it is one of Belgium's best-kept secrets, so there you go, we all need to stop there next time we are passing. Olive is happily motoring away from the wonderful Tournai at eighty-eight kilometres per hour, her favourite speed and so *Back to the Future*. Our motto is 'you may pass us, but you won't outlast us' and so far, this has rung very true. When we had our Best Breakdown Ever in 2012 on the way home from skiing in La Clusaz in France, the mechanic who fixed us up and got us back on the road sent us on our way with the daring prophesy 'she'll do five hundred/ six hundred thousand'. And I remind Will of those words every time he thinks the end has come. At that point Olive had only done three hundred thousand kilometres but since then she has had a 'new' engine fitted, so I am not sure anymore which bits of her will clock up the target six hundred thousand and which bits considerably less.

It was the Best Breakdown Ever, not because it was a minor problem but because what had seemed so desperate at 10.00pm on a dark road in the snow, went on to turn out so well thanks to some kind strangers who took us on as a project. The terrible clanking from her front wheel had forced us off the road into the haven of a restaurant car park. While Will phoned our mechanic back home for advice, I went into the restaurant and explained our plight to the owner. It was a quiet night for them, two days after New Year's Eve, so they had time to listen and offer a solution. Phone calls were made. First to a bed and breakfast, then to the wife of the owner who left her children to come pick us up (there were six of us, our two youngest Walt and Doris but also my mother and Will's brother) and drive us to the accommodation they had arranged for us. It must have been midnight when we arrived, but we were warmly welcomed and given two rooms, one with a double and one with a double and two singles. I cannot even remember who slept where, I just remember soft, warm beds away from the cold minus six temperatures outside.

We woke to views of Mont Blanc, in a village high on a hill. The owner of the B&B, Monsieur Bernard, had already contacted a garage and Olive had been picked up from the restaurant car park and was being looked over while we tucked into pain au chocolat, coffee and fruit for breakfast. Monsieur Bernard then drove Will down to find out the verdict. The problem was the wheel bearings, but they had some ordered and it would all be ready by the end of the day. There was nothing we could do but wait, so we had a look around the village and found that the only place of business in this tiny hamlet was, of course, a restaurant. This fine dining establishment was like a village hall with big windows high up on the wall, little decoration, plain tables and chairs and a tiled floor. The menu was a set menu with four courses including coffee, two choices per course and all for fourteen euros a head. It should be so much easier to negotiate a foreign menu and to choose when you only have two choices, but it all sounded so good it still warranted much discussion. Paté or salad to start, then steak or chicken with a choice of potato. Mousse or fruit to finish and then coffee. We ate alongside elderly couples, a family with a baby and workmen in plastered overalls. The atmosphere was functional; the food was fabulous; the price was perfect. And then we walked it off with a trek down the hill to collect our fixed vehicle. That was when the mechanic granted us many more thousands of kilometres in our beautiful yellow bus and we drove off, quite literally, into the sunset. Best Breakdown Ever! The cost? Okay so what with the B&B, the lunch, the repair and missing our Tunnel crossing by twenty-four hours, it probably added about five hundred pounds to the cost of the holiday. Worth every penny. We still pass the restaurant that took us in from the cold and helped us out; we remember the kindness of Monsieur Bernard, that wonderful lunch; and the words of that French mechanic are a constant soundtrack to our travels.

Back in Belgium we are 150 kilometres from Liege, twenty-five kilometres from Mons. We have just passed

Bernissart (Bernie's Art, we playfully rename it). This road has some horrible bumpy sections that do not appease the clanking from underneath. A Walter International lorry has just passed us, our first this trip. We have always had a fondness for them, what with our son being called Walter of course, and luckily, they are ubiquitous in Europe, so we see several on every journey we make. We have also driven past their base just outside Vienna and taken many a photo of our Walter stood in front of their distinctive blue and yellow trucks. Liege 133 kilometres. Ikea, also a distinctive blue and yellow, looms to our right. We travel to find the differences, but we cannot help taking comfort from the familiar. As we drive, we chat about mileage and map scales, the location of Maastricht and the lack of tolls so far. Once we get to Germany of course there are no tolls, but in France we have a clever thingy on our windscreen that activates the barrier at the tolls and bills us about a month later. It takes away some of the immediate holiday costs and makes us look cool. In recent years they have introduced one 'fast' lane where you can drive up to the barrier at thirty-five kilometres and it senses your thingy and opens with you hardly having had to slow up. It is the only time we are ever in a fast lane.

A Dutch caravanner pulls off the hard shoulder rather aggressively, causing Will to brake hard, but we do not retaliate with a toot. There is just no point – we are on holiday; we can afford to chill. A few drivers have beeped at us for no apparent reason and looked a bit angry as they passed by. We think it might be because of our GB sticker and the whole Brexit thing. They obviously have not noticed the 'Don't Blame Me, I Voted Stay' sticker in three different languages in the window. We do not want to leave Europe; we are *in* it.

It has been nearly two hours now and we are about eighty kilometres from Liege which means we will definitely be in Germany before bedtime. To reward ourselves for going so well we look for the next *aire de service* for a quick stop, coffee for the driver, petrol and liquid checks.

Hey, Walter International.

An *aire de service* is always a good place for some traveller watching too. Some people actively seek us out from interest in the look of Olive or maybe just fellow GB-ers come over to say hi and not have to feel bad about our lack of conversational French, German or whatever. Like Benjamin from Grimsby, driving a Swiss-plate car from his adoptive hometown in Germany, who worked for Converse in the week and managed a women's football team at weekends but was on his way to Vienna to manage a Slovenian rapper band (you cannot make this stuff up). Or we see something we cannot ignore like a litter of French Bulldog puppies spilling out from the boot of a car for their own pee stop. If they are in France though, are they just Bulldogs? One time a couple of young French guys in a tiny two-seater offered us some coke in a black holdall to carry across the border. I am embellishing this slightly to make us sound edgy – it was a case of Coca cola and an empty black bag that they just could not fit into their tiny car so were going to discard at the roadside. We hate waste so we accepted both items. The drinks did not last long, but we used that useful holdall for years.

The facilities of individual *aires de service* vary wildly from the architecturally interesting toilet block, clean enough to eat your brie in, to the ugly concrete shell with an enormous poo balanced on the toilet rim inside. The majority are perfectly useable, and you do not usually need your own toilet paper. For the record – Aire de Spy, cool name, nice stop.

Hey, Walter International.

During this stop, Will finally decides to get down underneath Olive and look for the source of the noise. He certainly finds it! The part of Olive that links the suspension with the steering and should be bolted securely in place has sheared off and is hanging loose underneath, swinging in the wind, clanking merrily. It was time for our first phone call (and it is only day one) to Ben. When he sees it is us phoning, he usually answers with, "What's fallen off?" Are we bad friends that we only call when we need help? Or are we good friends because we know he will help? And in fact, as we phone needing help a lot, there really is not much time left for non-help phone calls. Will takes a photo and sends it to Ben. Can it be fixed with wire or tape? If the answer is no, then it must be bad; nearly everything on that bus can be fixed with wire or tape. Alternator hanging off. Wire. Number plate fallen off but balanced precariously on the bumper. Wire. Broken wing mirror. Tape. We fix; we drive on. We keep going, further away from the UK and our AA coverage (they will not cover you in Europe if you are a certain age vehicle, which smacks of ageism). So, we keep driving and if we cannot fix it ourselves, we will try and find someone who can. The brilliance of the older car is that they are much more fixable than modern cars. No computer is needed to tell you what is wrong; you can usually see it, plain as day, hanging off, or you cannot see it because it is missing completely. And people like to help, and mechanics seem to have a great deal of respect for the VW Transporter/camper family. So far, touch wood, we have never been stuck.

Sometimes it requires a lot of people to help. One year, on the M3 in Hungary, while touring with our Hungarian friends, we had a tyre blow out. That is a shocking sound on any car – there is a bang like you've been shot at, then the car starts to slew all over the road. We were on our way to visit the Aggtelek Caves in the north-east of Hungary with Bali (pronounced like the fancy champagne not the country – bolly!) and his wife-to-be Aniko. They were in their own car in front, so we had to signal to them to stop and then get ourselves into the first parking area that came up. Luckily, it was not too far. Then the fun began. First Bali found the nearest garage and got them to be on standby for our arrival, with the correct tyres waiting. Meanwhile Will was trying to release the spare wheel, which is located under the bus near the front, held in place by a large metal frisbee bolted front and back. You could have put a gun to my head, and I would not have guessed where the spare wheel lived. It was not something I had ever given any thought to. The tool required to get that metal frisbee off could not get clearance from the ground to be used effectively. So, we needed to jack Olive up. Now, I do know where the jack lives – it is behind my seat. Unfortunately, the jack was too strong and the jacking point much corroded (this was pre-2014, before Ben got to work on the body of the bus) so instead of lifting it, it just started ripping through it. We needed another type of jack that would not be so brutal but still do the job. A truckload of workmen had turned up and were enjoying their lunch of bread, sausage and peppers. This is where Aniko stepped up. We needed someone who could speak Hungarian so obviously that counted us out. Bali was on the phone to the garage and frankly, the workmen would find Aniko harder to say no to. Aniko is exceptionally beautiful. And sweet. And lovely. So, we took a vote and unashamedly sent her over to the workmen. They immediately abandoned their lunch break and all five of them galloped over to help. Galloped. Sweaty, beardy Will would not have got such an immediate response, I am sure. They would have strolled over after finishing their repast at best. A trolley jack was produced; Olive was lifted enough for the bolts to be loosened; and the spare wheel was released. With some hearty 'thank yous' (*kersie* in Hungarian) to the workmen, we were back on the road, heading for the garage Bali had rung earlier to check that they had the correct tyres in stock, which amazingly, they did.

They did not. But, undeterred, one of the men jumped into a tiny Lada and drove off to a neighbouring garage who did have the correct tyres. He returned with four of them bouncing around in his car. While we were waiting the other mechanics had amused themselves by taking photos of each other sitting in the driving seat of Olive, laughing about it being on the 'wrong' side. Less than an hour later we had both front tyres replaced and a 'new' spare bolted back underneath, all for the princely sum of twelve thousand forints that equates to roughly thirty English pounds. So, thanks to two Hungarian friends, five workmen, one Lada-driving delivery man, the neighbouring garage, three tyre fitters and their boss, we were back on the road two hours after one tyre had blown out on the M3. It takes a village.

Anyway, back in Belgium 2017, there is just Will, Doris, me and the dog, not the village you want at that moment. But our best 'village' is on the phone. Ben's advice is drive straight, avoid potholes, no Evil Knieval stuff, cross fingers and all would be okay. I am shown the problem.

"See that one? It starts up there, curves round and is bolted on there."

"Errr yes, I see."

"Now look at this side."

"Okay, yes, I see, it's not bolted on there but hanging down onto that bit which is where the clanking is coming from but where it should be attached to?"

"Exactly!"

Usually, I just pretend I have seen the difference in the two bits of twisted metal or multitudes of wiring he is showing me just to stop having to look at something I do not understand. All I want to know is, are you going to fix it and how long will it take? But this time I really can see the problem, maybe because it is so frigging obvious. Can we get to our friends in Austria and fix it with power tools? A follow-up call to Ben puts that possibility out of the window. The part is only twenty-six pounds so do not try and bodge it, and more importantly, it cannot get any worse, so it is not irresponsible to continue. Maybe we can get it done properly in Hungary when we have more time? Spoiler alert – we do not bother and just drive all the way home with the clanking.

We are passing the exit to Huy, but we are not taking it this year, nor are we stopping at the upcoming Q8 services, best toilets ever and free to use. Not something to take for granted on the continent. Liege is twenty kilometres away.

Hey, Walter International.

We are seriously multitasking here, taking part in a quiz with Doris, avoiding potholes, refraining from Evil Knieval stunts and following signs to get us into Germany as quickly as possible. The signs are Verviers, then Malmedy and St Vith. It is 7.10pm; Prum is the town across the border; and we are passing Viaduct de Battice to our right. 1226 metres long, completed in 2007 as a high-speed rail bridge if anyone is interested. Twenty-five miles to the border on a nice straight road, smoothly cutting through a swathe of dense forest, the trees flash past as a ripple of texture, undulating across the landscape, snaking into Germany. There are some long, slow pulls up hills for us but mercifully no potholes. We pass the exit for Malmedy. We stopped here one year in an official sani-station that you are supposed to pay a few euros for, but we assume that is if you are using electricity, water and flushing your chemical toilet. Simple little Olive requires none of these facilities, so we squeezed her into a tiny space between two gigantic homes on wheels and left too early for anyone to have seen we were there. There was a wonderful bakery nearby for breakfast croissants and warm pain au chocolat. We stopped just outside of town to clean our teeth alfresco along the road.

Will is listening to the thrum of the engine and the many other noises the bus produces, trying to separate the innocent from the not so. I am busy with my maps and data and distance/time calculations as well as looking out of the windows. I definitely see more than anyone else – I see the deer in fields, horse riders, dog walkers, farm workers, huge buzzards on sentry duty along the motorway, tiny cars on distant roads, small towns as pockets of form and function surrounded by green fields and hills and forests. Doris is usually asleep or doing some puzzles though she is always keen for a good car game. The dog just sleeps. When we talk it is usually about the journey or previous journeys and often thinking ahead to the next journey. The call of the road is strong in us.

Germany

We cross into Germany at 8.00pm having driven about eight hundred kilometres already, but we are exactly where we hoped to be on our first night on the road. This is further than we have ever got before. We are in a forest as far as the eye can see, trees, trees and more trees, it is breathtakingly awesome. If you like trees. Which we do. It is a moment of sheer magic. We drink in the view.

Less magical is the realisation that the dog has peed on his cushion. That tells us that we have been driving for too long. However, Prum is twenty-two kilometres away and so, where there is civilization, there is usually a campsite. I have found a few marked on the map in that direction, so we plan to come off at the next exit and see what we can find. That exit is closed so we take the next one and immediately find a campsite sign as if it were meant to be. These are familiar signs to us, from so many travels in various European countries, blue with a white campervan and tent above. Often, they have an arrow and the name of a campsite which is especially brilliant when you are chasing a specific one and that is the sign you see. After a long day driving, these little victories can make a good day an excellent day. We are not looking for anywhere in particular, just a nice place to park up, turn off the engine and get ourselves into a shower. We find what we are looking for in a small village, down an unmade road (potholes!) opposite a sports centre. We park outside and I go into the reception office to make the initial contact. Do I speak German? I studied the German language for a year at school, back in 1984. I do not speak German. However, I know how to say 'do you speak English?' in about five languages and German is one of them. I can also say 'please' and 'thank you' and 'sorry' in most European languages including Hungarian. I can count to ten in German and Dutch, much further in French, to three in Italian and Spanish and, on a good day, to ten in Hungarian. I can fluently ask the way to the station in German and if it is located on the third street on the left, I might actually be able to find it too (weirdly this is the only bit of German my best friend from school knows too! We must have really been paying attention that day). We have a funny sticker on the bus window that says 'My German is a little rusty'. This is true on both its levels.

If you say 'Basil Fawlty' to anyone over the age of forty-five with reference to a person you may have encountered on your travels, they will understand that this is probably at a customer-based business with an owner/manager who seems to resent his customers for being there. We met such a character at another campsite in Germany, closer to Austria, and the resentment, I assume, was due to my inability to speak German and his unwillingness to speak English even though he quite clearly could. Who is at fault here is questionable. Is it me for not paying sufficient attention in German class all those years ago? Though I hope you'll agree I have a decent try. Or a man working in the tourist industry and refusing to use a skill he has mastered? The following is almost word for word what happened.

Me: "Hello." This is usually an acceptable opener in any language.

Him: no response even though I am standing two feet away in an otherwise empty, quiet office.

Me: "Hello." A little louder.

Him: "Hello." A little grudgingly I would say.

Me: "*Sprechen sie Englisch, bitte?*" Fluent German. Translation: 'do you speak English, please?'.

Him: "*Nein.*" Also, fluent German. Translation: 'No'.

Me: "Okay." A universally understood abbreviation. "*Camping eine nacht bitte?*" Translation: in my head this was the perfect way to ask for one night of camping.

Him: "Passport or ID *carte?*" Translation: either German is actually really easy, or he is speaking some English despite telling me he did not. But so far so good – we are communicating. And that is what matters.

Me: "Okay." I hand over our passports. Now this is where it started to go wrong because then he said something I could not understand; maybe it was too fast or he had a regional accent I was not familiar with, but whatever, I looked blankly at him and inadvertently made him mad.

Him: "What city are you from?" Translation: oh no, it does not need translating because he said it *in English*.

Me: "Gloucester."

Him: "Two persons?"

Me: "*Und eine kinder.*" Translation: 'and a child'. For some reason I am trying to win him back by continuing in terrible, halting German.

Him: "Three persons."

Me: "*Eine kinder.*" I only said that because sometimes that makes it cheaper.

Him: "Three persons." Obviously, children are people.

Me: "Okay."

Him: "Tent?"

Me: "No tent. And no electricity." Yes, I have given up butchering the German language at this point.

Him: "Electricity is included."

Me: "Okay."

Him: "Electricity and showers are included."

Me: "Do we need a token for the shower?"

Him: "Showers are automatic."

Me: "Okay, no token, that's good." It is probably hard to tell from this very mundane exchange, but the whole thing was bristling with hostility on his part and rising indignation on my part. I was fully prepared to tell him, in my best German of course, where to shove his campsite and his fluent and brilliant English, until he handed me the bill. It was sooo cheap. Just twenty-five euros for the night, for three, showers included, and although we do not need an electrical hook-up, we do, of course, charge our phones. Yes, you can get a decent night on a campsite for less than twenty, but you can also pay up to fifty euros and not get anything different than the patch of grass and a toilet block that you got the night before for half the price. So, I paid the money, said, "Danke," and, "Tchuss," and got the hell out. It was a really nice campsite; we got a lovely spot, had a great shower, met the neighbours, German on one side, Dutch on the other, and they could not have been friendlier. It was such a nice place at such a good price and in the perfect location, quite near the Austrian border, that we decided to stay there on our return journey too. This time, big fat coward that I am, I sent Will in with strict instructions to try and speak only German. Will chose Spanish for his year of an extra foreign language at school, so I gave him every German word I know, which did not take long, and the phrase book. What Will lacks in linguistic ability he makes up for in confidence. He boldly stepped into the reception office. Doris and I waited in the bus. We will never know exactly what happened in that office but after five minutes or so, I said to Doris, "Can you hear shouting?"

"Maybe it's Dad speaking German?" was Doris's theory.

It was not. It was 'Basil' shouting at him. In English.

"*I don't speak English!*"

Will came out looking shocked. Basil followed him to the door and was treated to the sight of me having to push Olive to start, as, annoyingly, she chose that moment to ignore the key. I hope he noticed it was a German non-starting bus. I pushed her all the way to our pitch. Our neighbours this time were a young English couple on their honeymoon in a hired VW transporter, G reg (ours is E), with square headlamps and LHD. They said he had been rude to them too. And that they were also ignoring their buzzer.

In 2017 though, we have Doris, at the midway stage of GCSEs and studying German, so although she had been no help with Basil back in 2015, she was keen to accompany me into the reception and try out her skills. She lets me start though, and with my perfect *sprechen sie Englisch, bitte?* the guy behind the desk admits he does, so we are off and running. His English is perfect, even though he answered 'a little' to my question. Maybe my perfectly accented German intimidated him?

So, we find ourselves, on our first night, in Germany, at Camping Bleiauff. It costs twenty-nine euros for the three of us plus the dog. This is a good price and, added to the eighty euros for petrol, just seven for food and two for a coffee, it has been a frugal day. We are already loving this campsite too. There is an enclosure by the reception with some birds and bunnies in it for the guests to look at, a small restaurant and a play area. The free shower block is right next to our designated parking spot, and it is a generous space to park and set out our table and chairs. When travelling with the kids when they were younger, one of the best moments of the day was, on arrival at a campsite, to release them from bus or bikes and leave them to it. It was their time to be let loose and they would disappear off to find playgrounds, animals, go-carts or just ride their bikes around. The dog is much more trouble. First, we need to sort out his pee-soaked cushion, get him fed and watered and then find the perfect spot to 'stake' him out on his long wire thingy. It cannot be far enough from us that he can bother other people, but we do not want him to be able to stick his nose into boiling pans. The wire is too long so we must double loop it through his collar. Once he is satisfied that the dog is in the perfect spot and the cushion has been rinsed of wee and set out to hopefully dry, then, and only then, Will gets the stove lit and the kettle boiling while I go and have a shower. I am a quick showerer and the kettle has a slow boil so I usually time it perfectly to be back for a cup of tea. Tonight though, it is quite late already so we are going straight for our evening meal. The first night's meal is always the same, wherever we go, whatever mode of transport, if we are self-catering, we take two packets of filled pasta, maybe some sauce, but after just five minutes of cooking it is a delicious, satisfying and easy meal. Tonight, we add pesto from a jar brought from home and some slivers of brie left over from lunch. After a long day travelling, this meal elicits the phrase from one of us, 'this is living', which means that something so simple has been made wonderful by the circumstances. A gourmet meal eaten in a field. I accompany my meal with my 'camping wine', a filled plastic glass with a foil lid. Next supermarket stop I will get a cheap bottle to refill the plastic glass as we go, but for a first night this will do me fine. Will has a cup of tea, Doris a hot water and we all have a mini Battenburg for dessert.

The deep rumble we heard earlier has turned into spots of rain. We leave the dirty dishes to their fate (nature's dishwasher) and jump into Olive with our drinks and the dog. The next half an hour is a satisfying time of trying to get battery lights to work, charging our phones on the portable charger, which also needs charging and, most importantly, trying to connect to the campsite Wi-Fi. All the time rain pounds down onto our roof.

And then it stops. Just long enough for us to hop out so Will can get the bed down. The back bench seat folds flat to 'meet' the front rear-facing bench seat. And that is it – it is very easy, but you need to move things in the boot away from the back of the back seat or it has nowhere to slide and then it is a bit of a pull and jerk mechanism that I find quite difficult so Will always does it. Once he has done that though, it is my job to 'make' the beds and cosy it up in there, so Will takes the dog for a walk and Doris goes for a shower. We sleep in a row, heads towards the boot end otherwise the lump where the two seats meet would be in your lower back/hip area rather than lower legs where it is less noticeable. We are all just too tall to sleep widthways, Doris and I only just but Will definitely. We sleep in sheet sleeping bags which are spare duvet covers, a single for Doris and a double for me and Will. We have lots of blankets for warmth and our own pillows and cushions. Everything is brightly coloured or mismatching florals, so it looks a bit like a nomad's tent with a multitude of wonderful colours and textures, and it is very cosy. Also, with just three of us, quite roomy. The dog sleeps on the front passenger seat harnessed to the seatbelt so he does not attempt to join us in the night. Normally he would also be on his cushion but of course that is outside now getting soaked in the rainstorm (nature's washing machine). The last time all six Greenwoods slept in the bus was in 2013. Although Maisie was twenty-three in 2013, she had flown out to meet us in Budapest and agreed to road trip back with us all. Some years previously Will's brother, Jonno, an excellent carpenter, had made us a very clever extra bed that looked like a stretcher, two poles and a piece of canvas, which balanced on the back of the rear-facing seat at one end but then had a clever stand at the boot end to hold it up to window level. We called it the 'mezzanine' and one of the kids could sleep on it while leaving a space free *under* it, sort of like a bunk bed. However, for the poor person underneath, it was a bit like being in a coffin. So, we raised the stand and made the 'mezzanine' higher which marginally improved things. It was always Will who got the short straw but that is because he is the dad, and dads are always the martyrs of the family. We are very sexist in our family when it comes to sleeping arrangements – wherever we are, the rule is, girls get comfort and privacy, if possible, before the boys. We also outnumber them, so they just have to lump it. This has resulted in Walt sleeping in a hammock strung across the width of the bus, out the windows and tied across the roof. He was about ten when he was able to do that but then he got a bit too big. He has also had to sleep on various floors, not always carpeted, though he did get some outdoor chair cushions to sleep on when it was a particularly cold tile floor at a holiday home in Hungary. He would have been perfectly fine if he had not made his bed in the way of a line of ants on their way to the kitchen in the middle of the night. His sisters were grudgingly sharing two single beds between the three of them, but, squashed as they were, they could see that they were better off than being trekked over by ants at 4.00am. The great thing about Walt though, is he truly does not mind. He can sleep anywhere, anytime, for as long as possible. He has fallen out of a top bunk and not woken up, though that may have been because he was knocked unconscious on the way down, I am not sure. He does say though, that he is awfully glad he has a girlfriend now, because when we all go away, she guarantees him a bed! We would never place the lovely Ashleigh in any kind of discomfort or in the line of fire… or ants!

Our beds are ready for the three of us; Will is back with the dog so we put him in his sleeping area and make a dash through the rain for final ablutions at the toilet block. Doris has stayed in there after her shower to charge her phone and enjoy the warmth. Back in Olive we notice a small leak under the rear window, but a plastic bag and some tape soon sorts that. I have put up the curtains. Only the ones on the right side stay up as we drive so every night, we have specially made 'curtains' that go across the boot and another one across the front behind the driver and passenger seats, so the dog is separate from us. He basically has his own room. There is also a huge curtain that starts at the passenger side window, tucks behind the visor, has a special hole for the rear-view mirror, tucks behind the driver's visor and then attaches to a knob at the end of the driver's side window. And lastly, a side curtain to go across the door. We are entirely enclosed, full privacy guaranteed and some protection to the morning sun waking us too early. Will sleeps nearest the door because he will get up first and go for a run with the dog; I am in the middle; and Doris is at the side. I would like to say we sleep well, but it is a very unforgiving mattress (now we travel more as just the two of us we have added a mattress from an old sofa bed to it and it is 100% better) but Will's back is aching from driving all day and I have woken up with a weird crick in my neck, and though the dog was quiet all night, the rain

Day One

made a terrible noise on the roof. We must have slept a little though because we were woken up at about 7.00am when the sun did start to leak through the curtains and other campers were up and moving around and some were even leaving already. Show-offs.

Day Two

You know you have woken up in Europe when the squirrels are red! We have seen two now, the first one in Hungary and now this one here in Germany. What a lovely start to the day, which we need because it is still raining. Packing up is hard because all the things we left outside are wet; the dog cushion with a little wee on it is now soaked through and we need to find places to put things. It is not the weather for a leisurely outdoor breakfast, so we just get on with the packing and get on the road. We have not even had a cup of tea so it was a good job we saw the red squirrel, or this day would be beyond saving. Will is a very easy-going chap, he is marvellous company, but boy does he get hangry! If we don't find a bakery, cafe or supermarket in the town, we will have to break one of our golden rules and buy food at the service stations on the motorway. Coffee and ice creams are the only exception to this rule. But if he does not get food soon, the driver is likely to cry! Luckily, he is distracted by the slightly bumpy road that will take us back to the motorway; he has potholes to avoid, so for now, his stomach is forgotten. And the road is calling. We drive through farmland and forests and another small town. Huge wind turbines stalk the landscape. The trees are sodden, and a damp mist hangs over the road, but the air is fresh and clean and pine-scented.

We are on the E42/A60 heading towards Trier, a single-lane motorway with an eighty kilometres per hour speed limit, but it is almost empty, so traffic is moving well. Some signs catch our eye, and though they are not ones pointing towards breakfast, they are funny. '*Ausfahrt*'. Yes, it is immature but yes, it is funny. We know it means 'exit' in German but still… it is funny. And more interesting than the Nimstal Bridge which we are just crossing, at 370 metres long it is an unimaginative piece of engineering and is so boring the driver has nodded off. He is veering so I give him a poke. He really needs coffee. Saarbrucken 139, Trier fifty-nine, both in the right direction, so we are well on our way across Germany, only about six hundred kilometres to Austria. That is quite a long time to be avoiding the police.

The first time we were stopped by the police in Germany was on that very first trip in 2006, so I am not even going to try and pretend that we were not a little alarmed when their vehicle pulled in front of us and 'Follow Me' scrolled across the sign on the roof. We had no idea why, or what we might have done, so it was a tense few minutes of driving as we followed them into the nearest rest place and parked up behind them. Both police officers got out and came up to the driver's side of the bus.

"Passports?"

Will looked at me and I scrambled into my bag like a frightened mouse to produce our six passports, handsomely attired in covers, so you could not even recognise them straight away as British (and let's not forget the British passport used to command a lot of respect – maybe not now). As soon as the police saw this wodge of documentation being waved at them their faces changed from stern to quizzical.

"Kinder?" one said, smiling, and peered into the back of the bus where four little faces peered back at him. And at that moment they realised we were obviously harmless. So, top tip for any future criminal activity: travel with children. They had to justify stopping us though, so they asked a few questions about where we had been and where we were going, had a quick look at our terrible packing in the boot and sent us on our way with quite a friendly goodbye. Phew, extreme relief all round. And then we realised we had a cool story to tell all our friends. Better than a tag on our toe. (Thanks Brad Pitt, *Thelma & Louise*).

We still drove away in a state of shock – being law-abiding citizens, we are not used to police interactions of that sort. And foreign police are way scarier; they carry guns. We were also wondering why we had been pulled over in the first place and why they seemed to change track when they saw the *kinder*. Was it that whole German v Britain thing? 1966? Was it a 'hippy' thing? At that time Olive was covered in large flower stickers. Is a 'hippy' thing even still a thing? This is not 1976. Maybe we were driving too slowly? That can sometimes make you look more suspicious. My friend Gwynn, who lives in Austria, has a theory. He thinks it is because one of the police officers can speak English and wants to show off to the other police officer. But neither of them had really spoken any English, so I do not give that theory much oxygen. However, about half an hour later, we think we might have got our answer. We were being overtaken by a *very* flowery campervan being driven by a *very* long-haired beardy guy, as opposed to our moderately flowered campervan driven by Will with his medium-length hair and neat holiday beard.

"Why didn't they stop that guy?" we asked each other while returning enthusiastic waves with 'that guy'. And then, because we are a bit thick, it was another hour or so before it dawned on us. They probably *had* meant to stop 'that guy' and they had stopped us by mistake, which was why they were so surprised to see the *kinder*. Doh, that does make some kind of sense. What are the odds? Two long-haired beardy guys driving flowery campers along the same stretch of German motorway at the same time.

The second time we were stopped was similar to the first – we were led off the motorway to a quiet road and parked up in a gateway, which was a little disconcerting as it was a lonely spot. More disconcerting though was when they asked for Will's driving licence, and we realised he had picked up mine by mistake (this was in the days of paper ones). We somehow got away with it and since then have been extra careful to take as many documents as possible. We still get it wrong though.

By the third time we were stopped, in 2010, we were fairly nonchalant about it all, but the fourth and, so far, the last time, in 2013 was the worst but, of course, the funniest. It was funny for Will after the event but for us it was bloody hilarious the entire time it was happening. If only we had had some popcorn, all we had to do was sit back and watch the drama unfold. It all began at a service station somewhere in Germany and everyone (all four kids were with us for this return journey from Hungary, Maisie having flown out to meet us there, while Meredith, Walt and Doris had done both legs) had gone to pee and get ice creams. Will had got some petrol and was parked in the large parking area behind the shop, waiting for us. He was killing time by investigating a greenish fluid that may or may not have been leaking out of the bus. A police car drove by, cruised past even, and very obviously slowed to check us out. We saw this as we were walking back to rejoin him. All they could see were Will's legs sticking out from under the bus, his investigations having taken him quite far under. They did not stop so we assumed they had continued onto the motorway. After Will had paid his fifty cents and had his wee, we started to drive out of the crowded parking area. Beyond this space was an even bigger parking area which was empty. This is where the police reappeared, like a shark lying in wait, and indicated to us to stop.

They were *not* friendly *at* all. No smiling, no lightening of the mood when they saw the charming *kinder*, no jokes about the bus. It was all business for them, the business of a supposed crime. First, they checked the paperwork. They were not happy that we had forgotten insurance documents, even though we had everything else, passports, driving licenses, the V5 and even a valid MOT certificate. They asked to look in the boot. Not sure what they hoped to find in there, but that seems to be a standard request. But then, and this is the best bit, they went rogue. One of them took a small plastic cup from a stack in their car, took off its wrapper and handed it to Will. With the help of some interesting mime work, they indicated to Will that they wanted him to pee in it, for, presumably, some kind of drugs test. The problem was, apart from being asked to pee on demand (at gunpoint is how Will tells this story), he had only just been to the loo at the services and got his full fifty cents worth so he just could not summon any up. Or down. Not even with the encouraging presence of an armed policeman standing a few feet behind him. Not a drop.

Back in the bus, we were watching this drama unfolding, imagining the headlines – 'Mild-Mannered Tee-Total Primary School Teacher in Drugs Scandal Abroad', while also warding off some dreadlocked hitchhikers who chose that moment to make their bid, until they realised they were about twenty feet away from some angry policemen (read the room guys). It is amazing how fast you can run in sandals. And, quite frankly, the five of us were mainly occupied with, ironically, pissing ourselves. We had no reason to be concerned; Will does not do drugs and has not even touched alcohol for fifteen years so we knew he was clean as a whistle. Unfortunately, the whistle was not performing so he could not prove it! Even after coming over and chugging a litre of water before returning to the cup with his policeman shadow – nothing. Clever chap that he is, though, he came up with an alternative – could they test his sweat? Because he had a lot of that. They said that yes that was possible so they took the cup off him and, times must be tough in the Bundespolizei, they *replaced* the cup in the stack. Now, fair enough it was unused, but it was not exactly 'untouched' if you get my drift, something had been... near it. If nothing else, surely once it was unwrapped it should be deemed unusable, but there it went, back in the stack. Ready for the next person. Will got his back swabbed and then could return to the bus while they waited in their car for the results. Maisie had managed to pap a photo of the back-swabbing moment and the way Will is holding his arms up makes it look like he is being arrested. This picture would make a great accompaniment to the headline 'Tainted Cup Police Scandal', or something a bit catchier. The test came back negative, of course, and we were allowed to continue on our way. So, when driving through Germany, we are always, always relieved to get into Austria. So far, we have never been stopped in Austria.

We are currently a long way from Austria though; it is nearly midday and we have not had breakfast yet. We have only been driving for an hour. We know it will take a long time for us to get across Germany because, as I might have mentioned already, it is an excessively big place, like it is showing off. Even with long stretches of empty roads and no speed limits in a thirty-five-year-old bus, you do not exactly eat up those kilometres. It is a lovely-looking country though, quite like England only bigger and greener and more foresty. And vineyards run riot over some of the hills. Other things are remarkably similar. Orange cones put in an appearance as a road closure takes us off the motorway and around Trier on some smaller roads, so it is all just trees, hills and birds of prey sitting on fence posts for kilometre after kilometre.

Hey, Walter International. First one of the day.

This stretch of motorway is devoid of services. So, no petrol, no coffee, no sustenance on offer for man or vehicle, and we need all three. That does not mean there are no stopping places; they are all just for parking which you know because they just have a big P on the signs with no other facilities mentioned. There are not even any signs telling you when the next services with petrol might be, which is unusual in this country known for its efficiency. But we are in wine country – *Moseltal* – and we are crossing a beautiful bridge spanning a wide river and a valley town. Our long bridge curves through the trees, past more vines, another valley and up and up and up. There are even signs for skiing, we are so high in the clouds. Finally, just as I identify a possible service station on the map, the next sign confirms it. Hochwald five kilometres. It is 12.45pm; Will needs coffee; Doris needs food; and the dog needs a wee stop. We break the rule about buying food (so much easier with one child than four!) and enjoy some tasty chicken schnitzel. We set off again at 1.35pm into the pouring rain. Now we need petrol. Maybe this is why it takes so long to get anywhere? We are really slow. And we stop a lot! Partly because Will only ever half fills the petrol tank because he is convinced there is a hole in it so if he fills it most of it will leak out. I am not entirely sure where this idea has originated but I let him have that one. It does not really matter because it is good to stop frequently, for the dog, for Olive, for our sanity. Olive has added a new tune to her song of the road – a weird swooshing metallic sound has joined the clanking symphony. I get told off for whistling because Will thinks it is coming from the bus herself. My whistling is not good, so I yield on that one.

Kaiserslautern seventy-six kilometres and the sun is out; the day is warming up; and the road ahead is smooth, flat and empty. If only life were a German motorway, it would be about perfect right now. Toll-free and no bumps, what more could you want? And we are feeling the love of our fellow travellers. At the campsite this morning, as I emerged from my cosy nest to make the damp traverse across to the toilets, a young man was walking by and called out, "I love your bus."

I responded with the classic British gambit of always referring to the weather by saying, "Yes it's great, thank you, just about kept the rain out hahaha."

To which *he* replied in kind with, "Yes, here in Germany we have just had one day of summer." And we continued with our days. I have no problem talking about the weather – it is the best way to engage with strangers because it always gives you something to say. I feel so sorry for the poor folk who live in places like California, where it is sunny all the time; there cannot be anything to say to the old lady in front of you in the queue at the post office. Fellow Europeans get it though; we have real weather. It probably would have been nicer to talk more about how fabulous Olive was but again, my go-to had been to be self-deprecating and talk about leaks. You can take the girl out of the UK, but you just cannot take the UK out of the girl.

At the services Will has recognised a Dutch car by the bikes on the back because it had overtaken us a couple of times (they must stop more than us!), and he looks at bikes on racks, so he says hi and compliments the couple in the car on their bikes and they, in turn, compliment Olive. It is all very lovely. Not so lovely is the strong smell of burning coming from Olive which we are hoping is just the brakes getting hot and burning off some of the wet from all the rain that has fallen in the last two days. This happened once before on a steep potholed (!) road in Hungary and we had to keep stopping to cool down the brake discs. When we ran out of water, we used squash which made them sticky and a little hyperactive, thanks to all those pesky E-numbers. We have also had real fireworks in the cab but never an actual fire, though we do carry a fire extinguisher just in case. The battery is located behind the driver's seat in a sort of box with a metal lid on it. For as long as we have owned Olive there has been an old, ripped piece of cardboard under that lid. We never thought about its purpose until it got moved and the metal lid touched the contacts of the battery and sparks flew. That is where we keep the Haynes manual now, which is the best use for it that we have found.

We have changed roads now and the petrol situation is becoming desperate, so the plan is to go off at the next junction and find somewhere, anywhere. There is a sign for an air base, so my logic is saying *petrol*; then we see the golden arches of McD's on the left and again I think *petrol*, but then there is an actual petrol station on the right so that seems a much better call. Storks have built a nest on the McDonald's sign and are standing up there guarding it. Not something you see in Croydon. Forty-five euros of petrol later (yes okay, and a couple of burgers, we could not resist that golden M) and we are back on the road, sun streaming through the window, enjoying the smooth tarmac and commenting on how we have not seen any other GB cars for a while. The road ahead rolls up and down the hills in a vaguely hypnotic way. The famous lack of a speed limit does not affect us in the slightest; we have our own limit – it is called thirty-five-year-old bus, but someone has just passed us at a crazy speed. Like something out of a cartoon, with its own sonic boom sound effect.

The junction for Bad Dürkheim has just come up. We have stayed in this town a couple of times. The first time was after a long, hot day of travelling and we were desperate for a shower. We did not find a campsite sign when we drove into the little town, but we did find a supermarket and at the supermarket we found a kind lady who told us to follow her and led us to a lovely version of a sani-station in a large field with plenty of room, some trees for shade but no facilities at all. It was nice, and it was free, and normally it would be perfect for our needs, but this day had been so hot, and we really needed showers. We politely thanked the kind lady but as soon as she was out of sight, we hightailed it out of there to follow some campsite signs we had spotted when we first started tailing her. This was a big, fancy lakeside campsite with cars parked outside and barriers to go through to get to a shiny reception block, with prices to match. But the showers were free, clean and hot, so it was worth every penny. We got a spot next to the lake and everyone had a swim in that too. Our neighbours were a single gentleman in an ordinary estate car made into a camper with curtains and a mattress and a young couple in a truck with a tent on the roof. We were an odd bunch.

We have stayed in Bad Dürkheim twice more since and both times used the free camping the kind lady showed us the first time. It is a good spot if you do not need a shower (and we have now added a solar shower to our pack list) and can walk five minutes to the public toilets in the town square or find a bush if you are desperate. The town itself is an interesting place, a pretty, orderly German town, all amenities well signposted and remarkable for two rather unusual tourist attractions. The Giant Cask is the largest wine cask in the world with a volume of 1,700,000 litres, though sadly there is not that amount of wine in it because it is a restaurant. The other thing is a very odd thing – I still don't really understand what it is and what it does, but I shall try to explain. It is a graduation tower which is a large structure used to produce salt, removing water from a saline solution by evaporation. It dates from 1736 and is a huge wooden frame stuffed with bundles of brushwood. It looks like a giant version of one of those insect houses you can buy in garden centres. The brushwood is changed after five to ten years due to encrustation. Just walking around it and breathing in the mineral-rich droplets in the air is supposed to be beneficial to your health. It is huge – at 330 metres long it is one of the biggest in Germany (there's more than one?). We have walked round it each time we have been there, marvelling at the structure, the colossus of it and the basic mechanics of the system, but I still do not really understand what it does and how. Will has explained it to me each time, but it feels a bit like when he tries to show me how to read a dipstick. I just don't get it.

We are not stopping in Bad Dürkheim this year because of our earlier start and first night already in Germany instead of Belgium – we are at a different stage in the journey than we normally are. E31 – following signs to Speyer. Heilbronn is 107 kilometres away. At 3.30pm we stop for some lunch and enjoy our bread and cheese in a services parking area. We drive on at 4.20pm. There is a strong smell of onions coming through the vents and then we see the groups of workers in the fields picking them. This is the point we pass the thousand-kilometre mark for this trip and go from eye-watering onions to breathtaking bridges, a red and blue cable-stayed bridge. The 1970's 'modern' look of blue 'wishbones' with red cables fanning down against the bright blue cloudless sky, it could be a sculpture in a park not a functional piece of engineering. Spectacular. Nimstal Bridge take note – this is a bridge! Heilbronn 62 – this is a nice bit of motorway we are on here, easy to track our course on a map. German exits are numbered in numerical order rather than the Austrian system of using exits as distance markers from the big cities. Nurnberg, or Nuremberg as we know it – 209 kilometres. Our first traffic queue. Roadworks have caused us to lose a lane, but we are moving slowly as drivers continue to use all the available space and merge in turn. It works well and we are not held up for too long. We start gathering speed again, but it is too soon, and Will has to brake sharply. Lemon slices fly across the cab area (for our European-style tea with no milk of course, not a gin and tonic). Olive is moving out around the blockage, and we are beginning to increase our speed. Will checks what is ahead, the speed of the lorries but also an oncoming hill, gauging speed and distance. Can we risk an overtaking manoeuvre? The lorries will slow on the hill but so will we. We're doing it! We're overtaking! Come on, Olive! A Hungarian car has just gone past, first one we have seen. Follow that car. A man has also just gone past texting with both hands! He must be steering with his knees.

We are passing Sinsheim, home to an aircraft museum, which, if you stretch your neck as you pass, you can get a glimpse of the original Air France Concorde, brought over from Paris in 2003 after it retired. I have a fondness for Concorde as its distinctive shape flew over my 1970's childhood home in Kent every evening at 6.00am on its way to the London airports, disturbing many a game of 40/40 as we all stopped playing to watch it go. We also stopped for something to eat in Sinsheim once, which is not something we do often so that is why I remember it so well. We found a lovely restaurant in a beautiful old building where they sat us at a huge round table. We had steaks English style, which means rare, which was odd to us because we thought we had a reputation for overcooked meat, some huge pizzas for the kids and a free dessert in a toy truck for the youngest member of the family, Doris. I cannot imagine that the French would refer to rare steak as English style unless, because they like their meat *bleu*, they do consider rare to be overcooked. Food for thought. Also, final Sinsheim fact: it was one of the host cities for the Women's World Cup in 2011 and again in 2019. I highly recommend a visit there.

Hey, Walter International.

The sky is dark blue, and the pressure is dropping. More rain? By the side of the road, amongst some newly planted trees, are what can only be tall wooden bird perches. They are posts with triangular tops for the birds to perch on. We always see large buzzards evenly spaced out along the motorway, so we do not quite understand why they need to be encouraged in this way. Is the motorway at risk from a tiny rodent infestation? Will it get chewed through? Seems unlikely but anything to help wildlife is to be applauded. Any efforts for nature to cross the road carefully is also to be encouraged. There are some funny little bridges we see across a particular motorway in France that have trees on them, so it looks like the trees are crossing from one side of the forest to the other. I love that. A6/E50, passing Heilbronn, there are long lines of lorries confined to one lane and doing sixty kilometres per hour so we, even we, can pass them. Talking of lorries, we have just passed a famous lay-by in Greenwood family history. We call it 'Trucker Piss Stop'. One time we had stopped there for the usual liquid checks; in fact, this may have been where Will left the oil cap the time that resulted in the appropriation of a Nescafe lid to replace it. As he got out of Olive, amongst other things, he noticed a small puddle under the front bumper, possibly the result of something leaking out. So, of course, he got down on his knees to investigate, thinking to himself, *oil? Coolant? Petrol?* He got just close enough to get a whiff of it and immediately jumped back up to his feet.

"Trucker piss," he declared emphatically and then waited for the laughter to erupt around him and for the gentle bullying to start.

"Dad tasted trucker piss!" The actual truth of it being just a quick sniff never needed to get in the way of a good taunt or a family legend.

A beautiful town opens out to the left with, not one, but two onion dome churches. To our English eyes, used to grey, square, Norman churches, these Russian-inspired spires seem very exotic and far too fancy for Germanic Germany.

Hey, Walter International.

Out the window more pastures, vine-covered hills and enormous wood stacks next to balconied Alpine-style houses.

Hey, Walter International.

And a wee stop for all, including the dog. The driver is exhausted, so he is closing his eyes and taking a personal moment while Doris and I play with the dog, until Doris states that she thinks she has appendicitis. It is great fun travelling with these two. Thank goodness for the dog – apart from pissing himself, he is a dream travel companion. We are now all laughing at me having said that, so the mood in the bus has lifted. It is true though that we do spend large portions of the day in our own bubbles. I will be reading the map, looking out of the window and writing this journal, taking care to record all of my hilarious jokes. Will listens to music through earphones which helps to keep him awake, or he listens to Olive and all her weird noises. Doris is asleep 90% of the time or she is on her phone. Olive is a noisy beast and as Doris sits on the rear bench seat, it can be hard to communicate with her sometimes, but we have enjoyed a spirited game of I Spy or the counting game, in which one person thinks of something you might see a few of, for example, car transporters, and then counts them as they see them while everyone else must guess what they might be counting. To our chagrin, our kids do not often take much notice of what is going on outside the window unless it is for a game. We have driven through some stunning landscapes and mostly they are on their phones, playing cards, sleeping, reading (Maisie only) or bickering. Some sights are more engaging than others – there is a tunnel you emerge from on the way to skiing and suddenly there are the snow-capped mountains in the distance ahead of you, or arriving in the city of Salzburg, or following the Danube through Budapest past the Parliament building. These are all 'wow' moments if you appreciate that kind of thing, though experience has taught us that, apparently, you have to be 'old' to do that, i.e. over forty. One time they were all taking note of their surroundings was the night we arrived at Hotel Castle Dracula in Transylvania in an actual friggin' electric storm – some of us were very scared. And the whole way along the Transfagarasan Highway in Romania – they absolutely loved that, though traffic was bad. Behind us. No one was on their phones for those parts of the journey, though I do remember some bickering.

We plan to drive for another hour and then start looking for a campsite. We form this plan while crossing the Ornthal Bridge – 241 metres long and fourteen metres high. As good a place as any to make a plan.

Hey, Walter International.

Nuremberg 141 kilometres. Traffic has slowed to a crawl. So, while we are not moving there is time to reflect on the hilarity of seeing '*Gute fahrt*' on signs ('good driving') and how so many places have 'Bad' ('Bath') in front of them, which is also funny. Our favourite is Bad Waltersburg which of course we translate to Naughty Walters Town. It's the little things...

These signs confuse Will because he is so slow at reading that he can only read the first bit as he drives past, so he only sees the 'Bad' bit on the sign, so if you are looking for a specific town starting with 'Bad', he will try to turn off at the first one he sees which may not be the correct one. His poor reading skills really let him down in Germany.

Day Two

It is raining now but we have just seen a P registration go by which is, of course, sunny Portugal. Will's watch is recording the pressure at 915mb so we discuss what that means, and I impress him by using the word parameter correctly. We are also discussing how the dog does not really 'get' camping because if we are outside of the house, he thinks it is all about him, walking, peeing, chasing balls, pooing. That is what 'outside' is for. We are also crossing the highest bridge in Germany, Kochertalbruge, at 185 metres high, 1,128 metres long and 410 metres above sea level. So, is that highest in height or highest in the country? As it mentions sea level, I am going with the latter. Nuremberg is still 113 kilometres away. Junction fifty-two shows a possible campsite option by a lake. Traffic is crawling along as we lose a lane, going from two to one. It is not roadworks so it could be an accident, which is confirmed when we pass a lorry with blown-out tyres and traffic begins to speed up. New plan: junction forty-eight E43/A7 camping at Oberwornitz about twenty kilometres away. Another tyre blowout and everyone is slowing down to avoid the debris.

Now we are taking junction forty-eight, and this is the best part of the day when we are chasing down our bed for the night using only a symbol marked on a map. When we see the blue sign with the white arrow, it is like the pot of gold. Then, you find it and it looks nice, and reception is open, and a friendly face welcomes you and says there is a space and showers are free and it costs less than thirty euros – well, it just doesn't get any better than that. And that is exactly how it turned out! Even better, we got to it on the Romantic Road (we would say we travel everywhere on that). The campsite is a large, grassy area surrounded by trees, a few static mobile homes, but not too many, and a neat little reception. Our kind of place. Doris and I manage the entire transaction in faultless German with the nice man behind the counter, though he slipped into English a couple of times to help us out or, possibly, for his own practice. I am sure he was unimpressed with our linguistic skills, but he must have appreciated the effort.

For now, we have arrived, time to pick out the perfect pitch, with the right gradient for ultimate comfortable sleeping. We drive around a couple of times and move back and forth a bit to get the exact right spot. Will patiently puts up with my vagaries on this, but I like to get it just right. Then we get the stove going, stake out the dog and hit the showers. The shower block is yellow with flower beds around it, and there is a bar but no shop. Breakfast is tomorrow's problem. We have our supper, classic second night choice of tinned curry (more delicious than it sounds) and boil-in-the-bag rice. Then it starts raining again so while the other two go and shower, I settle in the open boot, cosy after my own shower, ready for bed, to read the guide to the Romantic Road that I bought in reception. I had planned to do the washing-up but then the heavens had opened, complete with thunder and forked lightning, so shelter seemed the best option, with a glass of wine and an interesting book. The washing-up can wait. A good book cannot. The Romantic Road is a route from the River Maine to the Alps. It sounds lovely. It would be great to do it one day and write a book about it. I spilled a bit of curry water from the cooking pan in the boot, but I am putting it all outside to be washed up in nature's dishwasher and the mess I made is quickly mopped up before the spillage police can see it. He is extremely strict about that sort of thing but then, this bus is our home. We need to get the beds down, secure the dog in his 'room' and play a few rounds of cards before sleep hits us like a sledgehammer.

Day Three

We wake up to beautiful sunshine at 6.00am when the dog manages to scramble over the passenger seat and invade our bed space despite being harnessed to the front seatbelt. We shoo him back into his own sleeping quarters and he stays put until gone 8.00am. At this more civilized hour, I get up and stake him outside, and we both have a morning wee. His is executed right there on the grass, mine in the campsite facilities. I envy his freedom. Then, Will emerges in his running vest and shorts and takes the dog for his morning run. No movement from Doris. I start the breakfast machine, which is so much easier when it is sunny. Sitting outside, making the tea and enjoying some cereal is a vastly different experience to the previous day, stuck inside the bus surrounded by wet stuff.

During breakfast we are disturbed by a crashing sound in the trees outside of the campsite fence. The dog starts whimpering and squeaking, which only means one thing: squirrels. He loves chasing squirrels more than he loves chasing tennis balls, and he desperately wants to join in with the chase now, but he would have experienced his usual squirrel chasing frustration because these guys were not coming down to ground level. And what a pair! One was red, so that was brilliant, but the other one was black! Maybe it was very dark grey, but it looked black from where we were sitting. We have seen black squirrels in Canada, but we did not know they could be in Northern Europe. Poor old red squirrels are at the mercy of the grey and the black as those two carry a pox that can decimate the red squirrel population. No wonder this one was running. They both disappear into the treetops and the dog finally calms down. How many I Spy points for a red squirrel? And how many for a black one? Will knows these things – only this morning he had returned from his run with 150 points for having seen not one, not two, but three Roman snails, worth fifty points each. In the world of I Spy, this is a big score.

We pack up and set off at 11.00am, intending to stop at the Aldi we had passed coming in yesterday. We will not make it all the way to Gwynn and Elke's tonight, so we will need a supper and some lunch. Plus, some pain au chocolat and brioche for brunch. And some sweets. And I need wine. Unfortunately, we left the motorway at one junction and have rejoined it at a different one, so no Aldi. We are on the E50/A6 heading towards Nuremberg and beyond. The road is bumpy enough to warrant cursing from the driver but at least it stops him thinking about food. I ask him how he remembers about the Roman snails. He says it is because that was the most points for anything in his I Spy Creepie Crawlies, but he never saw one in the whole of his country-bumpkin childhood. The first place he did see one was, strangely, at the Chedworth Roman Villa in Gloucestershire. They are like snails on steroids as they are huge with a thick shell.

Regensburg 150 kilometres. That is the last big place on the map before Austria so we will definitely be in Austria tonight. Some Swiss and Austrian number plates pass us, so we get a bit excited. Soon they will all be Austrian.

Playmobil Fun Park next exit. That sounds amazing! But we do not stop there; we stop for boring old petrol, coffee, croissants and a dog wee. I bought some reading sunglasses for this trip, and they are great for map reading, but if I look up to read the signs, I cannot see a thing. I must swap them for normal sunglasses, so I have a bit of a juggling act going on. Will is busy trying to merge out of the parking area back onto the motorway, which is always difficult for the right-side driver. Lorry drivers are always considerate, caravanners not so much.

There is a lot of road building going on in Germany – a few times we have been shepherded onto the wrong side of the road or down to one lane because a whole new section of road is being created. It is done with minimum fuss and great efficiency. That is not quite how it was when we visited Romania in 2015.

Romanian Detour
(On paper not in reality!)

I am sure that someone famous, illustrious, definitely literary and most probably dead once said 'when one embarks on a road trip, one rather expects that there will be roads'. Romania had other ideas. Romania subscribed to Doc Brown's 'where we are going, we don't need roads!'

We crossed the border from Hungary at 5.40pm, which was actually 6.40pm, though we did not know at this point that Romania was another hour ahead of the rest of Europe. Travelling into another time zone, and we had to show passports at the border, so this was serious road tripping. Then we had to immediately stop to buy a vignette to drive on the roads. We were already slightly freaked out by how many of the road signs were leading to places in Russia. We are intrepid road trippers, albeit in a scaredy-cat, mild way, but Romania was definitely as far east as we wanted to go. Ever. I read one thing in a guidebook for Bulgaria warning of dodgy cops making up fines on the spot, and that was enough for me; with our history of police stoppages there was no way we were going to invite trouble. And I once considered whether we could drive up through Finland to get to St Petersburg, but then I read some stuff about how that might go down with the locals and it very much put me off. Olive attracts a lot of attention anyway, as would a GB sticker, and we just don't need the hassle, although it would be worth it for the adventure. Maybe one day, but this was scary enough for now, being in some shanty town no man's land at the border in the fading daylight queuing at an assortment of dilapidated shacks trying to buy the vignette while avoiding shady characters wanting to sell us mobile phones. It was dirty and hot and mildly threatening (we are superwimps when it comes to that sort of thing and have no wish to become part of some sort of *Taken* scenario – despite Will having a particular set of skills, they mainly involve tape and wire, or explaining fractions) – so it was a huge relief when he returned after being gone for nearly half an hour waving the vignette triumphantly. What a gigantic waste of paper that would turn out to be.

The road we needed to take to get us to our first night's booked accommodation (again too scared to just wing it!) was missing one entire side of it, so we were subjected to lengthy stops at temporary traffic lights while two miles of traffic came the other way. The side of the road that did exist was just one pothole after another. In that first evening, slowly easing our aching, creaking bus over every lump and bump, we managed to drive just forty kilometres in about two hours. There was no way we were going to make it to our booked campsite. We would have to gird our loins and wing it.

Which turned out brilliantly. Hooray for winging it! Not so scary after all, maybe we could go to Russia? We stopped at the Pensiona La Migu and, in faltering 'Romanian', got a two-room 'apartment' for the five of us (we had Walt and Meredith with us on this trip too) for just twenty pounds. This is when we found out about the time zone difference, that Romania is an extra hour ahead of Hungary, which meant that the kitchen would be closing for food orders an hour earlier than we thought. With watches adjusted accordingly, we made it down to the restaurant with half an hour to spare, to enjoy some chicken and chips, with bread and salad, and cold Cokes all round for an incredibly reasonable price, similar to the cost of our room for the night. I still remember that meal, on our first night in a new country, and how great it tasted. And, after a long day travelling – when things seemed to be going so wrong, with the roads, not being able to get to our booked campsite, the extra hour and how late it really was – to be sat there, with full stomachs, coffee ordered and a bed waiting, my family safe and happy, was deeply satisfying. All was right in our world.

Day Three

We returned to our 'apartment' where everyone had their own bed, even Walt, and slept soundly until we were woken in the morning by barking dogs, mooing cows and a buzzing chainsaw (!). Of course, breakfast was lovely and included in the price of the 'apartment'.

The roads continued to be the nemesis of the bus on the second day in Romania, forcing slow speeds and wince-inducing clunks from the undercarriage. While Will fretted about repairs, I tried to console him with the idea that any one of the farms we were passing would have spare parts and welding equipment and the know-how to fix anything. This old bus from South Africa was built for this kind of shit! He remained unconvinced, knowing the frailties of Olive better than I do. What we have always found, though, is that out here, at the eastern end of Central Europe, they know the value of fixing things.

Except, it seems, their bloody roads. We passed workmen digging with pickaxes or shovels but not a mechanical digger in sight. It was extremely hot that summer in Romania, mid to high forties every day, so it was quite common in the middle hours of the day, from 10.00am until 4.00pm, to see groups of workmen asleep in the shade of a tree. In three hours, we drove a meagre seventy kilometres. Only the blackberry lady could save the awfulness of that journey. She was not another mobile phone seller but an old lady in classic Romanian apron and headscarf selling actual blackberries at the side of the road. In the most spontaneous action I have ever witnessed him make, Will swung Olive off the road and stopped next to her. We all gratefully exited the sweltering bus and approached the lady who was smiling a toothless smile at us. *Suckers!* she was probably thinking. No, I am sure she wasn't because the next twenty minutes was just lovely in a slightly embarrassing 'look how charming the locals are' kind of way. But as much as we like to tell the story of how we bought a ton of blackberries from the Romanian lady without a single word of a shared language and yet a satisfactory communication from both parties, I expect she also entertained her husband that evening over their cabbage rolls with her own tale of the pale, sweaty family from distant lands with a huge appetite for blackberries. As much as she absolutely made our day that little bit brighter, I like to think we enriched hers (well, we literally did because we gave her money for a fruit that we pick for free at home).

Finally, we hit an actual motorway and it was *lovely* – long, straight, smooth and completely *empty*! Romania had, at that time, just 176 miles of motorway in the whole country. We were extremely happy to be on that small section of it. Will was beaming. We drove 117 kilometres to the town of Sibiu and had another delicious, and cheap, meal in a restaurant on the town square surrounded by gothic, medieval and renaissance architecture. A stunning backdrop for another great meal. This was the only time in our lives we sat in a restaurant without having checked the menu and prices first. We also slept that night in a corporate motel, and it was on the drive there in the early evening dusk, as I saw a bat lazily flap away from us, that the actual realisation hit me: *I am in Transylvania and it is night-time.*

Slept well. No weird dreams. I knew I would be safe though because I packed my wooden stake (I'm not even joking – I have one that I keep by the bed. Will made it for me). Here in Romania, I was fulfilling a lifelong fascination/obsession/fear with vampires. I was 'into' vampires before it was trendy; I cannot even remember the film I must have seen to trigger it, probably a *Hammer House of Horror* masterpiece that was on one Saturday night in the '70s, but from a ridiculously young age, I have always slept with the duvet up to my chin and the windows shut no matter what the temperature. I can just about have the window open now as a rational adult because I reason that when (not if) they do come in, hopefully, they will get Will first. Mosquitos always do so why not vampires? He obviously has much tastier blood than me. You only have to say the name Danny Glick and that's it, I will not sleep that night. I like my vampires properly gothic, old school and bloodthirsty, none of these newfangled, out-in-daylight, seem-quite-human excuses for the undead. Romania had 'real' vampires in the shape of Vlad Tepes, and we visited his lifetime haunts, Poenari Fortress and Bran Castle. I touched walls that Vlad may have brushed against as he rushed to fight off the Turks. And then there was the fictional Dracula. On a dark and stormy night, we drove up the Borga Pass through the town of Bistrita where Jonathan Harker spent the night before travelling on to Castle Dracula. It was renamed Bistritz in the novel. By the time we were approaching the castle it was dark; the road was lonely – it wound through mountains and forests – and there was an actual electric storm going on that was so atmospheric we wondered if it was a special effect put on by the hotel to freak their guests out. I was wondering it, not sure if anyone else was that gullible.

Hotel Castle Dracula is a modern-looking hotel with gothic overtones built on the exact spot where Bram Stoker wrote it as being. We knew it was the right place because it said it in blood-red lighting on the side (gulp). Lightning flashed across the sky and illuminated our way across the car park to an enormous studded wooden door (double gulp). We had to open it ourselves, no hunchbacked manservant did it for us. Inside, the reception area was decorated with stuffed animals and low-hanging candelabras of *exactly* the kind Peter Cushing would have swung on to tear down the curtains and transform Christopher Lee to dust (huge gulp).

Meredith went straight to bed as she was already feeling unwell, even before the night of expected bloodletting. Will, Walt, Doris and I went to the half-empty, enormous dining room with a lot of windows (so many points of entry!) and ate a meal of meat and onions and peppers impaled on swords. It was brilliant, food and a weapon in one. A foot and a half high, one sword between two. A superb feast, perfectly suited to the setting. And then it was bedtime. Now we were going to have to try and sleep in this place. We accompanied Walt down the corridor to the room he was sharing with Meredith. For some reason he was slightly unwilling to go there alone. Meredith was in there, sleeping peacefully, with the windows fully open and the long, white curtains fluttering into the room on a gentle breeze. Meredith's beautiful, dark red hair was spread out on the white pillow, framing her pale face. She did not stir when we entered. Sleeping so deeply, you could barely see her breathing. On her perfectly white nightie, a single drop of blood made a stain on the collar.

I'm kidding! There was no blood – she was just sleeping – and she's always pale. We said goodnight to Walt and left him to close those windows and get into bed. It had been a long, hot day and we were all exhausted.

I did not sleep a wink. Partly because it was *so* hot and especially so with the duvet tucked under my chin for protection. After a few hours of this, I reasoned that a duvet was not much protection and that the sleeping form of Will closest to the window was probably my best chance of surviving the night. And my stake under the pillow of course. I am not completely mad, but I do have a vivid imagination, and vampires have been under my skin and in my brain for too long now to be dislodged by reason or maturity. What I was really worried about was that it may be gimmick put on by the hotel, to scare their guests to death in the night. Although that probably would not get you great reviews on Tripadvisor. I just did not want to hear any scratching on the window. That's all.

I must have slept a little despite all the crazy in my head because I remember opening my eyes to sunshine and breathing a sigh of relief that day had dawned. On flinging open the curtains I saw how I had slept so peacefully. On the hillside opposite was an enormous crucifix. I am a devout atheist but, in that moment, I would believe anything you want me to.

That hotel was without a doubt the best hotel we have ever stayed in. Generous-sized rooms, comfortable beds, clean, efficient showers in luxury bathrooms and great food. Two rooms, dinner for four and breakfast for five cost less than a hundred pounds.

We were beginning to really fall for Romania, the people we met, the food we ate and the prices we were paying, combined with such beautiful cities and interesting landscapes. We were seeing some amazing places and experiencing moments that have not changed in five hundred years. Every evening as we drove through the villages, we got caught up in the daily ritual of bringing the cows in from the fields. Some were in small herds of five or six or maybe a dozen; often it was one cow on the end of a rope following one head scarfed old lady or a mortified teenager. People still drove horses and light traps instead of cars and it became a familiar sight to see them 'parked' outside shops and houses, looking as out of place to us as the Amish look in America.

We drove Olive up the Transfagarasan Highway, the road built by Ceausescu in the early '70s as a response to the 1968 invasion of Czechoslovakia by the Soviet Union. It winds its way across the Carpathian Mountains and connects Transylvania and Wallachia with the purpose of being able to move military forces quickly if under threat. We just wanted to take Olive on a road that *Top Gear* called 'the best road in the world'. We feel a bit guilty that we may have ruined it for any supercars stuck behind us, but we had a great time. We stopped at the 'honey man' halfway up to buy some of his golden honey from the bees in his portable hives (off the back of his lorry). We ate our lunch in another scenic spot and our fellow picnickers shared their peppers, bread and lard (to be eaten on the bread) with us. Everyone was so friendly. Meeting Alex was an absolute highlight. We were looking for a hotel and walked into his. It was full, but he showed us the way to his other hotel and set us up in two rooms there but also insisted we return to the first hotel to have dinner in the restaurant. Another fabulous meal, traditional dishes but also some more simple options for the less adventurous palate. The chefs came out to meet us, grinning and bowing at our attempts to compliment them in Romanian. We returned there in the morning for breakfast which included some of the biggest pancakes you have ever seen. Doris was in heaven! On that journey we bought pine squash from another head scarfed lady at the side of the road; we watched Will drink sour yoghurt thinking it was milk; we stopped at cafes for drinks and ice creams just because we were hot. This country was both exotic and familiar; the telegraph poles look the same, but these ones have storks nesting on them, and not just one or two but whole streets of them.

There was one Belgian Flyover moment, though I have not got to the story that explains this phrase yet, but basically it is a moment of despair and desperation. It came on the potholed excuse for a road leading to Viscri, a World Heritage site in Brasov County, Transylvania. Will had brought Olive to a halt to have a break from the jolting, plus, some of the passengers had heat and hormone-induced stomach issues (it was forty-three degrees) that required a roadside dash to some bushes. The worry was that Olive too was close to spilling *her* guts out at the side of the road. But we lurched on, stomachs and bus alike, to Viscri, one of the oldest villages in Romania. Children, dogs and chickens wandered the unmade streets. We passed the magnificent, fortified thirteenth-century church with barely a glance, the Saxon houses, of which King Charles owns two, garnered only a flicker of interest, we just wanted to get onto a smooth road and stop feeling sick. Just outside the village, still bumping along an unpaved road, just as we got to a makeshift wooden bridge, Olive died. She gave no warning, just cut her engine. Within seconds, a vanload of men appeared on the road behind us and three jumped out to push us *off* the road so *they* could continue on their way. We, on the other hand, were stuck. Not to be outdone, Doris, Walt and I jumped out and started to push. Meredith relocated to the front seat to give moral support to Will. With a supreme effort he was able to bump-start the engine and we too could carry on along the unmade road. Leaving the side door open just in case we needed to jump out again but mainly because, even in the cooling evening, it was still so hot, Doris and I sat with our legs dangling out of the door, bare feet catching any breeze we could. We passed some simple concrete houses, in clusters of two or three, with brightly painted exteriors and most of life's living done outside. We waved to the children watching us pass by, to the women hanging out the washing and the men tending to livestock, and we hope that they saw the spirit of the Romany in us too, and for a brief moment we were as much a part of the landscape as they were.

End Of Romanian Detour

Back in Germany in 2017, we needed a supermarket, so our only choice was to get off the motorway so we could stick to our number-one rule of never buying food at service stations. *Never*. Except ice creams. And coffee. And we did get that chicken schnitzel the other day. But with only those exceptions, the rule stands firm. The motorway is a bit of a mess anyway, more roadworks, narrowed lanes, signs crossed out and exits closed. We have one 'phew' moment while passing a tanker that seemed to be closing in on us, intent on crushing us against the concrete blocks. Apart from that, we pass through smoothly. This is the sort of thing that would cause a five-mile tailback in the UK, but you have to remind yourself that we have significantly less space and just as many cars in it. I still think that Germans just know how to merge better.

Various motorways cross at Nurnberg, so we say goodbye to the six and join the three. There is a lot of history connected to Nurnberg, or Nuremberg to us, but we have never actually been there. So much of the medieval town was destroyed in the war, 90% of it lost in one hour, two thousand citizens killed. Like Gdansk, the city was rebuilt after the war and restored as much as possible to its pre-war appearance. One day we absolutely must take the turn off the motorway and look for ourselves. We add it to the list that already has Tournai on it.

Junction ninety-one to Berg or Neumarkt should lead us to a supermarket and lunch. It is two hundred kilometres to Passau which is basically Austria. The heat inside Olive is considerable, so when we do find a Netto in Berg with the modern joy of air conditioning, our shopping takes quite a while. Especially down the fruit and veg aisle where the produce is kept fresh with water misters. It is funny how long it can take you sometimes to choose an apple. After lunch is bought, air is put in tyres and petrol station facilities are used, we now need to find a good lunch spot. We want a parking area with a lot of shade, so we just keep driving until we find one. Passau is now only 149 kilometres, so it takes us fifty kilometres to find the perfect spot. But eventually we do and enjoy our lunch of brie and ham rolls, red pepper, crisps and fruit. And fifty points to me, I see a Roman snail at the lunch spot.

Next stop will be in Austria, though that is not strictly true as we will have to stop just before to buy the motorway vignette as only Germany offers free motorway driving in all of the Europe we are planning to drive through. Belgium does not seem to charge tolls on roads, or at least not on the ones we have been on, but we have paid to go through a tunnel before in Belgium and also in the Netherlands. France has its tolls of course, but we have our 'thingy'. Austria, Hungary, Romania and Switzerland all require a vignette. I cannot remember about Croatia, but Slovenia also does because we had to buy one there despite being in the country for only a few hours. We only went there, though, so we could say we drove through an extra, previously unknown country on our journey home. We have since returned, in 2019, and it is a beautiful place and well worth the vignette money. Anyway, as I said at the beginning, this is not a guidebook so please check the laws and requirements of the countries you intend to drive in before you set off. Or you can just find out en route as we often do. They all make for a fine collage on your windscreen to show off when you get home.

Passau 111 kilometres. Nestled amongst the green hills, rising out of the vineyards are two distinctive structures.

Day Three

One is the golden arches of McDonald's, the other the orange turrets of a monastery, welcome sights for the weary traveller in both modern and medieval times. A car transporter passes us carrying its load of small, white cars, possibly Fiats, with 'Grow Up' written along their sides. We take these messages seriously. We once saw a campervan in Holland with 'Not Normal' painted in huge letters all down the non-door side. We have that as our family motto now. Partly because, in the same holiday, an irate campsite owner had accused us of being just that because we let a child pee in a bush. We had just arrived; we didn't know where the toilets were; and she was only four and couldn't hold it any longer. Not the worst crime in the world, is it? But the opposite of normal apparently. We'll take that.

An Albanian car passes us. Passau is now only seventy-seven kilometres; it is hot; everything is sticky; and our bodies are slowly cooking in this moving oven. With the windows open it is very, very noisy. The police overtake us and pull in front. No communication, but they do not attempt to overtake the next car so we just sit behind them, wondering if they are wondering if they can be bothered to pull us over. But they exit at the services, and we drive on, staring ahead as if we hadn't even noticed them. Phew though. They were probably discussing what ice creams they should get at the services and were oblivious to our existence.

German villages and towns are easy to spot from the motorway because of two quite distinctive features: onion dome churches and orange tiled roofs. In the UK, you might spot a church spire needling up above the trees towards the heavens, but the houses themselves tend to blend into the background. In Germany, the churches are often yellow and the houses pink, blue or green. There is an awfully big river dissecting this countryside too. The road crosses the Donau for the second time. We know it as the Danube, and we will 'follow' it in a less meandering way to see it again in Budapest. It is wide and serious, and it links our trip through Germany and Austria to Hungary. It is bigger than that though, flowing through ten countries into the Black Sea. It is the second longest river in Europe at 2,860 kilometres long, beaten by the Volga at 3,690 kilometres long. We get a friendly toot from a lorry driver to say thank you for letting him out even though he had already given us the classic 'thank you' light flash of left indicator, right indicator, or a quick touch on the hazards. There is a language of the road, and it is non-verbal so works for all, but it helps if the driver is sitting on the 'right' side of the car. Will gives him a cheery wave back, but we do not think he sees it because he is not expecting it to come from the right. Sometimes I like to loll my feet out of my side window to freak out the drivers behind who will assume I am the driver. Our Hungarian friend, Geri, taught me that.

We are slowing down past an enormous field of sunflowers, alas not to admire the view but because the road is narrowing again.

Hey, Walter International. Not seen one for a while.

And we cross the Danube again before stopping at Donautel services to buy the vignette for eight euros ninety cents, get ice creams and liquid checks for dog, driver and bus. The dog gets a few licks of an ice cream too. It is 5.15pm, the time I estimated we would cross into Austria, but we are still about half an hour away, so I stay on the Deutschland map until we see a border sign.

Austria

In my head I think of Passau as a little watchman's hut on the border, watching for carriages galloping between the two countries, shutting a gate to stop them to check their 'papers'. It is a romantic image of a pass into the next country, though the reality is a metal sign with the blue background and gold stars of the EU and Österreich written across the centre. It is 6.00pm exactly, and we are in Austria.

Austria. Cows. *The Sound of Music*. Mountains and skiing. Edelweiss and strudel. So many favourite things in Austria. Also, we are out of Germany without having alerted the constabulary to our presence. We have done some people watching at the services though. There were some men praying on mats on the grass verges between the cars, some young women lying in the sun on mats, doing a different kind of worship, and there were a few large families sitting at several picnic benches having, what looked like, a three-course meal. We noticed another VW like ours, with German 'Will', dreadlocked 'me', no 'Doris' but a dog. There was a rather splendid, silver French van with folding side doors that two kids roller-skated out of. They were wearing jumpers on this swelteringly hot day! Their dad immediately lifted the bonnet but then sat on a three-legged stool to look at his map while having a smoke. He was either really bothered about the journey or not bothered at all. Will falls somewhere between those two states. He does not lift the bonnet (we do not have one; the engine is under the luggage) nor does he just sit and smoke and ponder. He does a full liquid check at every stop, and it is probably this diligence that, remember, though other cars may pass us, they will not outlast us.

The road is smooth into Austria as it exits Germany but quickly turns a little lumpy. The silver French van with the roller skating kids (now inside it, not hanging onto the bumper!) passes us and we exchange friendly waves. Model cows stand in a field next to the road in the Austrian flag colours with *a faire milch* painted on them. Are they an advert or a protest? A 'Keep Your Distance' sign depicts two crumpled number plates as if in a collision. One is Austrian; the other is German. Oo-er.

The countryside here in the north is flat and pretty, though not as dramatic as the mountains in the south around Salzburg and Innsbruck. It is time for us to find a campsite and we know exactly where we want to be. We follow a smooth, winding road away from the motorway across farmland to the pretty town of Aschach an der Donau, which lines the banks of the Danube with pastel-coloured and gold-lettered Baroque– and Renaissance-style buildings. Just out of the town, on a riverside plot, is the most perfectly located campsite we have ever been to. We stayed here in 2008 and promised ourselves we would return and, finally, nearly ten years later, we have (and we would return in 2019 too). Finding the campsite is easy because the road goes no further than it. You can only continue on foot or bike, or boat. As you enter the campsite there are neat permanent caravans with proper gardens and patios which lead to a huge chalet-style hotel and restaurant with a spacious grassy area in front for the tourers. In 2008 we were lucky enough to be in the first row with only the river in front of us but this time we must content ourselves with the second tier. In reception I recognise the lady who greeted us nine years ago. That time I mistakenly used the Dutch word for two instead of the German which was annoying because I am good at one to ten, it is about all I can do in those languages, and I got it wrong. This time I have Doris and her GCSE German with me. She bravely has a go at doing the entire conversation in German and the man behind the counter professes himself impressed with that and that we were also return visitors. But who wouldn't want to come back here? It is gorgeous. Our host comes outside to see Olive, so I show him the photo I had taken of us there in 2008. Same place, same bus, two extra kids (Walt and Meredith), all a lot younger. Great price (twenty-four euros), great showers, under the hotel itself so 'indoor'. And, of course, an amazing location. When we get somewhere like that, we often lament that it is for one night only but honestly, once you have drunk it all in and had one evening sat out under the stars with a glass of wine, in utter peace and contentment, you might as well move on to the next piece of sublime. That is why we travel, because we are always looking for the next perfect spot. It does not mean you cannot return to the good ones though.

It is so quiet here – the river flows past; occasionally there is a swish of bike wheels; boats go by silently, even enormous river cruisers don't make a sound; and the rockface on the opposite bank deadens what noise there is. The dog takes a dip in the Danube (not a bad life for a rescue dog from Dublin) and chases the ducks until they all turn round and start chasing him. It is very comical. He has swum out quite far and we worry that he is in the shipping channel so Will goes into the water to entice him back with the promise of a ball throw. Will wades out thirty, forty, fifty metres and it is still only waist deep. The dog is chasing swans now at more like a hundred metres from shore. He is also swimming down river so is getting further from where we are. I follow him on the path, keeping an eye on his bobbing head. He is attracting some attention from the 'locals' and I hear *eine hund schwimmen* from a few of them. I cannot tell if it is said in awe of his supreme athleticism or a judgement on our irresponsibility. At about three hundred metres from where he started, and about 150 metres out from the shore, we get him back by throwing sticks in the water. He swims over whimpering in excitement at the idea of a stick game; Will hauls him out; he has a shake, then goes for the stick and tries to jump back in. You would think he would be exhausted but no, he is ready for another paddle; in his mind those swans won't chase themselves. We shake our heads at him so he knows that although we think he is an awesome dude who could probably outswim a shark, we have to show that his behaviour is not acceptable. We have a theory that this is how he turned up in England needing a new home, because he swam across from Ireland! The reality is that he came across in a Dogs Trust van, but our story is cooler. Though our version would mean there might be some nice Irish family looking out across the Irish sea wondering where their lovely dog went. Here in Austria, a neat place with many rules and regulations, we worry that some of the other campers may be thinking we are very foolish to have endangered his life in such a manner. We put him on the lead and head back for some food, some Olive appreciation from our neighbours and bed.

Day Four

We have a dear friend from Gloucester who now lives in Austria with his Austrian wife and their young son. Since that very first journey in 2006 we have always popped in and stayed for at least two nights. In 2017 this would be our first visit with the dog in tow, so we plan to impose for only one night in case he does not get on with the resident dogs. Our dog is a sweetie with humans, but, partly due to his advancing years, he is not particularly interested in other dogs, especially young pups. They annoy him and he is not afraid to let them know it. It is not particularly aggressive behaviour but the natural way that older pack members keep the youngsters in their place. He tries to ignore them but, if necessary, he will turn on them with a growl and the canine equivalent of a clip around the ears. He is a Staffie cross and a possible street dog from Ireland so he can handle himself just fine in the face of dog aggression. He once growled at a fellow Staffie as we passed in the street and the owner said to him, "I wouldn't if I were you." *Well, he already has*, I felt like replying. But I didn't because they both looked very threatening. I just thought it. Quietly. I assume that our dog weighed up the threat and knew a growl was in order, so the other dog knew not to mess? I cannot pretend to understand 'dog', but it seemed clear to me that he knew what he was doing. As with most Staffies he is very mild mannered and would definitely just roll on his back for his tummy to be tickled if an intruder ever entered our house. Unless they brought a dog with them. Then he might bark. His ferocious-looking 'I Live Here' picture in our window has to suffice for our security. So far it is working. Despite the pretty flowers in the background of the photo, he still looks like a threat.

Anyway, I had phoned Gwynn and told him we would arrive at lunchtime, which could be any time between 12.00pm and 4.00pm for us, but, by 11.00am we have still not left Aschach because it is so beautiful and restful and peaceful, and also because it was so bloody hot, we couldn't quite face getting into the bus. Will and the dog had been back in the Danube, tied together by the running lead so no more swan worrying for the dog. Or Will. We enjoy a leisurely breakfast and then finally pack up. The journey to our friends should take about two hours and bring us right to the Hungarian border. If we can just drag ourselves away from this beauty spot and dodge Danube touring cyclists who come at us on the narrow roadway like Space Invaders. We are keen cycle tourers too, so we show them no animosity for their road hog ways. Cyclists are more common than cars on this road; they even have a dedicated tile sculpture of a bearded cyclist on the edge of the riverside path. Will is on super high alert for some reason; his meerkat sense is on overload (thanks to an ongoing tinnitus condition he is extremely sensitive to noise) as planes roar overhead.

Doris's phone jangles and I accidently squirt him with spray sunscreen while he is trying to drive. We nearly miss the sign to Wien (Vienna) so indicate a bit late and an Austrian driver honks at us and won't let us in. Where's the love?

We are on the A1 to Wien and our exit is St Polten at 109 kilometres, junction seventeen to Baden to cut the corner off. We pass a familiar landmark, the giant red chair advertising XXXLutz furniture store. As usual we are the only car on the road with the windows open. There is no other air conditioning in this old bus. When I told a friend that we were planning to drive to Hungary in 2006, that was his first concern for us. My response has now become family legend, "We have windows that wind down." Olive has also joined nature's dishwasher with her own wing mirror washing line and dashboard dryer. Basically, there are pants everywhere.

The motorway is lined with windbreaks of different materials and designs. Some are clear, with those bird stickers on them. Others are wooden with huge, wooden fruits appliqued on them. There are more patriotic cows, and not just for Austria but France, the Netherlands, Germany, Belgium and the European Union. A United Nations of milk. It makes us feel sad that we are out of that loop now.

Mountains loom to the right, close enough to look pretty but far enough away to not worry Olive with the prospect of a climb.

Hey, Walter International times two. And a Wolter Koops, also yellow and blue but Dutch in origin. We also see a Dorys every now and then. It is fun, like our own family I Spy, and can include that cat food in Aldi that was named after me too. Another family joke is that William is not a common name because, of all of us – Juliet, Maisie, Meredith, Walter and Doris – his *is* the most common, although Maisie might be catching him up. So, we always comment and point out when we see William on any lorries, shops or signs. These kinds of capers help the kilometres go by. We take a short break at Ybbs (no idea how you pronounce that – 'ib'?) *raststation* for petrol and an ice cream because it is now thirty-six degrees and rising. Olive is feeling it too. After thrumming along sounding like a sewing machine for days now, suddenly the old nightmare of lights flashing and temperature gauge rising forces us to pull over for a cool down. Last time the temperature needle shot off the scale like that it was because the alternator had fallen off. The needle went so far up it did not reappear for a few days. Will checks the levels but it is hard to get an oil reading because it is so hot the oil is bubbling up the dipstick. After the brief rest, we continue, and the temperature remains steady, but we are backfiring like popcorn in a microwave. But you would, wouldn't you, if you had hot oil running through your parts? It is just as if Olive has eaten a vindaloo. And now there are hills. Big hills, this is Austria after all, they even have a song about their hills. This means a hard pull for our heavy, old, hot bus. The temperature is sky high but beginning to come down as air flows through on the downhills. We are not air-cooled but it helps. We are not going to make Gwynn's for lunch as it is now 2.30pm but maybe afternoon tea? Or supper.

We have been in this situation many times and, to be fair, she keeps on going – the wheels keep turning even when they sound like they are about to fall off (wheel bearings); the gauges issue their warnings (hot bus, hot oil, no alternator); and even when it once seemed like the entire engine had seized up, Will fixed it with water, a simple solution he applies to the many other ailments using wire, tape, a bent paperclip, nuts and bolts, and so we carry on; we watch the levels; and we hope. And not just hope but have faith too. I have a lot of faith in Will to use his certain skills, in our mechanics back home and in the old-school German engineering know-how that built this bus. I have faith in our dumb luck – things have always worked out for us; we have found help or what we need or come up with a great bodge. We are a good team. Will worries; I calm him. He can be a bit negative; I am super positive, and we meet somewhere in the middle. I often say to him, "What's the worst that can happen?" Well, I suppose we could get stuck in the middle of nowhere with a bus that will not move, but this is Europe – you cannot be too far from somewhere. All problems can be solved by throwing money at them. This might not be what you want to do but that is what credit cards are for! We have only needed a bailout once from the credit card and a generous parent, and that was for the Best Breakdown Ever, so totally worth it. This is the worst thing in Will's world, having to spend money. For me, I worry about being crushed between two lorries or plunging off a narrow mountain road. That sort of overimaginative catastrophe never even enters Will's head. That is why we are a good team.

Hey, Walter International.

This is the worst aspect of road tripping, when we drive in silence, me trying to keep the faith, Will watching his

Day Four

dials and listening to every sound Olive makes. If he makes a noise of exclamation and I ask him what that means, he can get cross, thinking that I do not understand the seriousness of the situation. Today is so hot, even with air flow, putting your arm out of the window is like taking it out of a pan of boiling water and putting it into an oven. There is poor relief from the heat inside Olive. She is stuttering and backfiring up the hills and even the shimmering cityscape of Vienna opening up ahead of us cannot detract from the desperation. Vienna looks hot and bothered too. It is downhill though, and we are twenty-five kilometres from sanctuary.

The oil warning light is on all the time now so Will does the trick he used to do with the buzzer: turns off the engine at speed and bump-starts it back on to reboot the systems. It works for a few minutes but soon comes back on. Is this the new buzzer? Will this light never dim? I cannot see the dials from way over here in the passenger seat, so I have to ask what is happening and this increases the tension in the bus. Which is not fair because I am just as interested in a safe arrival as the driver is. But he is so worried that he does not want to verbalise his fears.

Hey Walter International. Hey Walter International. Hey Walter International. Hey Walter International. Hey Walter International. Hey Walter International. Hey Walter International.

We are passing the *home* of Walter International as we move onto the A2. It is a sprawling depot from where all Walter International lorries are born. Usually, we are excited to see it – it is a great landmark for us but also seeing our son's name in ten-feet-high lettering standing out boldly against the blue Austrian sky is quite a thrill too. Today however, it gives no relief from hammering down an ugly stretch of motorway in the blistering heat in a bus that is about to explode. Or melt. Sandra Bullock knows what that feels like. It is thirty-eight degrees. We are twelve minutes away and then we will have thirty-six hours of no driving. We do not speak; Doris is asleep anyway and we are just staring at the road ahead, willing for the exit sign to come up next. Junction thirty-eight and then it is literally five minutes from there. Olive doesn't know she only has a few more miles to toil before a well-earned rest. Last time we made this exit and came up off the motorway to a small roundabout, the accelerator pedal detached from its mooring; we lost power and slowly drifted to a halt on the road but luckily, directly opposite a petrol station. I immediately jumped out and started to push – it was not a busy intersection, but two cars appeared behind, assessed the situation, pulled over and two ladies, independent of each other, jumped out and joined me in the pushing. This combined womanpower, plus Will pushing and steering from the driver's door, got us out of the way and onto the petrol station forecourt. The kind ladies probably thought we had run out of petrol so made no further enquiry into our wellbeing and, after some sincere thanks from us, returned to their cars and went on with their days. We were left with a flapping accelerator pedal. Of course, Will fixed it so we could make the final mile to our friends and while we were there made a more permanent fix with some tools and a new bolt.

This time, however, we smoothly glided around the roundabout, if lurching and backfiring can be described as a smooth glide, found the correct right turn for our friend's street and quietly, without ceremony, but a lot of relief, turned off the engine. Phew. 4.20pm, six hours after setting off on our two-and-a-half-hour journey, we had arrived. In a little place called Wiener Neustadt, less than twenty kilometres from the Hungarian border and home to Gwynn and Elke and Alex.

I met Gwynn in 1995 when I worked in a pub, and he came in just before last orders every night for a quick pint of John Smiths before bed. We became friends and when he met Elke on the internet and moved to Austria we stayed in touch. Then Alex was born. This will be our sixth visit to them as we pass by on the way to Hungary. We love staying with them because they are super hosts. We eat well, drink well and sleep well when we are with them. The only payment? A four pack of John Smiths and some marmite from 'home'.

Elke is a woman after my own heart. For her there are so many interesting opportunities and projects to explore. One year we arrived to find the garden turned over to ten chickens and a dozen quails. An egg industry was in full swing. But two years later the birds had gone after complaints from the neighbours and been replaced by two enormous and extremely unruly dogs. They were bearded collies – 'dogs that do not look like dogs' is how Gwynn described them. For Elke's greatest project is her family, and because her two unruly boys, Gwynn and Alex, were not getting much exercise, she decided that having dogs to walk every day was the remedy to that. Elke throws herself into new plans with great energy and passion. So, to get a dog, she drove to Poland, as you do, to get exactly the right one from exactly the right breeder. On arrival, said dog bounded up to her and knocked her flying. Even this ignominious start could not put Elke off her master plan. Recognising a kindred spirit matching her for enthusiasm, she bought this dog and brought it home. I am not entirely sure how a second one got added to the family but two they have and both of them whirl round the house and garden like canine dervishes with topknots so they can see and yet still bashing into anyone who gets in their way. It is a house of no rules for dogs and children alike which makes it great fun to visit. Doris adores the trampoline, the above-ground swimming pool and the free Wi-Fi.

The dogs were acquired as a way of including some exercise into their otherwise sedentary life – Gwynn's favourite pastimes of bird spotting, nature watching and photography all necessitate sitting very, very still for long periods of time. Gwynn doesn't even have to leave his garden to do these things; he has made some legendary (amongst a select band of fellow nature enthusiasts on the internet) 'spots' from his own garden. Alex is a typical teenage boy, already towering over us at age thirteen and preferring computer games to anything outdoors. He once said to us, "I can't run very well," while watching Doris bounding up and down some tree stumps on a hill in a natural playground, "but I don't need to." Which we thought was fair enough, who does actually *need* to run?

Healthy eating was also part of the health kick as all the family had gained some weight thanks to Elke's superb cooking. She devised a diet which consisted of one day of fruit and veg only and the next day of 'whatever you like', which is no more a ridiculous diet plan than some that are popular. It was never going to work though, because on his 'whatever' days Alex would have cake for breakfast, washed down with SodaStream Cola. But maybe we should all eat like this because Alex is a genius. Fluent in two languages (he has to translate for his dad, who has picked up extraordinarily little German in fifteen years of living there), he is a superbrain who thinks a little differently to everyone else. He is probably going to be the next Bill Gates. His favourite computer game on this particular visit was one to do with office management. The 'game' was to manage an office space, the staff and the business. No one in this game got shot, attacked by zombies or had to drive a car really fast. When Will pointed out the sleeping caretaker in the basement, suggesting he should be fired, Alex replied that as he got paid by the task not the hour, it was not a problem. Alex is very funny, sometimes unintentionally – he has no filter, but he is great company and we have enjoyed seeing him grow up in two-year increments. He enjoys our visits too and, when he was younger, would cry at our departure.

Gwynn quietly lets the chaos of this family life that he arrived at a little later than most wash around him, utterly content, completely happy, often bemused and, sometimes, downright bamboozled. Surrounded by the animals, plants, craft projects, Amazon deliveries, bulk buys, SodaStream and cake, he sits in the garden, as much a part of the scenery as a giant gnome, watching the birds and photographing insects. We hope to continue to visit and share this wonderful existence in their beautiful corner of Austria, even for just forty-eight hours, for many years to come. They once told us that our visit was the highlight of their summer. The feeling, dear friends, is mutual.

Day Five

But short and sweet is the key to a successful visit so we leave after just one night, with a bounty of food for the journey, some cold drinks and this time, quail eggs. Goodbye friends ("Goodbye free Wi-Fi," Doris whispers). The day is a little cooler after a rainstorm last night, so Olive is happier. We are heading south before we cross into Hungary because this time, we are going straight to the Balcsi, as Lake Balaton is known to the locals, an endearment for the largest lake in Europe because the Hungarians love it so much. As a landlocked country this is their seaside.

Usually, we go up and across to Sopron, so close to Austria that Austrians go there for shopping and dental care. We also stopped there once, to make a start on the enormous lunch Elke had packed for us. It is very beautiful in the way of old Hungarian towns, cobbled streets, large squares, tall buildings and pavement restaurants. When we head to Budapest on this route, we also pass Sarvar (both these towns start with a 'shh' sound). This has to be the Mecca for any true vampire enthusiast. Forget Transylvania – here is the castle of the only actual documented vampire, as a possible drinker of human blood, the Countess Erszabet

Bartory. Allegedly, she thought that drinking virginal blood kept her youthful. This was before Botox of course, and you tell me which is weirder, injecting yourself with poison or drinking the blood of a virgin? For her trial they gathered the testimonies of over three hundred witnesses, including survivors and imprisoned girls found at the time of her arrest in 1610. They collected physical evidence from the horribly mutilated dead and dying stacked in her cellars. Because she was of the nobility, she escaped execution but was confined to a tiny cell 'walled up' until her death in 1614. Whether actual vampire or extremely prolific murderess, that was reason enough to visit her castle. You need to be able to read Hungarian to understand the exhibits in the museum and, judging from the names in the visitors' book, they saw no need to translate them. I was happy to walk in her footsteps, touch walls she may have touched, go up steps and through doorways her skirts may have rustled through. Drink in the atmosphere of a much older Europe where wolves still howl in the forests, superstitions are real and maybe things really do go bump in the night. And a new family game was born, saying Erszabet in a screechy, high-pitched doll voice at creepy moments, like setting off in the dark to clean your teeth in campsite toilets or on arrival at Dracula's castle. Brilliant game. Meredith was particularly skilful at choosing the right moment and executing it in the right tone, Walt particularly creeped out by it. Let the big sis little bro teasing commence.

Today though, we are heading towards Graz on a motorway so Olive can hum down a long, straight road at a steady eighty-eight kilometres per hour, then we will cut across to Szombathely which is over the Hungarian border. The scenery here is beautiful: classic Austria, hills turning into mountains, blue skies with low-lying white clouds, forests and farmland. Inside the bus the oil light is flashing but the temperature reading is fine, so we ignore it and drive on past red-roofed white houses and white churches scattered down hillsides like a handful of dice. We are entering Thermenland (land of spas?) and travelling the lovely smooth road that is the A2, passing Bad Waltersdorf, which makes us think of our good Walter, who by now has flown out with his older sisters to Budapest and should currently be staying with our friends until they meet us at the Balcsi in a few hours' time.

It comes to something when the fact that, though a piece of your vehicle's steering/suspension mechanism is unattached and swinging in the wind, that is the least of your worries. We have not done a single Evil Knieval stunt, so we know we are keeping our promise to Ben. It is the bloody oil warning light and overheating worries that occupy us now. I know that an engine can overheat and seize up because it has happened before. Though it was not actually seized because that time Will was able to fix it with water. We were trying to find our friends' newly built house by driving down a series of unmade roads amongst many other newly built houses that of course satnav had no knowledge of. The roads were made of sand; it had been another long, hot day; and it was extremely frustrating to literally be so near yet so far. Once more, Olive decided to die. I think she just does it for attention. Will was certain that her engine was completely seized up and that that was the end of Olive (or at least, that engine). After a few minutes to cool down (him and Olive), he tried the 'pour on water' trick and it worked! We were on the road (sorry sandy excuse for a road) again.

We are on much smaller roads now but nothing too lumpy or bumpy or hilly. And definitely not sand! When we stop for petrol, it is still in euros, so we are not in Hungary yet. It is only 10.15am and we are slowly moving through a large retail park at Furstenfeld with some interesting shop names – Takko is our favourite and the very 'woke' Mister Lady. Then we are in the countryside, cornfields and villages, lots of yellow, white and orange, cyclists and sunflowers, supermarkets and flowered bridges. There are bright pops of colour and signs we can still understand, *'reite'*, *'links'*, *'gastehaus'*. Until 11.00am when we cross the border. The road is dustier and bumpier; there are border checks but no barbed wire, and we cannot read *anything*. Welcome to Hungary.

Hungary

So, this is it. Hungary. What do we know about Hungary? Prior to 2005, not very much, mainly facts to do with vampires – Bela Lugosi, who played Dracula in the earliest film of the book, was Hungarian, Elizabeth Bathory (Erzsebet) Countess Dracula of course and Transylvania used to be part of Hungary. Some things were household names even in 1970's Britain, so we knew about biros, goulash and Rubik's cubes, but that was about it. I do not think we felt like we needed to know any more. After 2005 though, we did. We learned about the origins of their strange language; we knew which side they were on in

Day Five

the war (the bad side); we knew about communism and what happened in 1956; we could talk about the great era of Hungarian football and about Liszt. We know there is a Grand Prix; we know more food now, like their famous paprika, *langos* (a sort of batter served with sour cream), *palascinta* (tiny thin pancakes), Pálinka (a very strong spirit) and that they absolutely love fish soup. And of course, I remembered about the Austro-Hungarian Empire from my history classes. It is probably for the best at the moment to not dwell on their politics and enjoy this interesting, beautiful and extremely hospitable country for its people. But that could be said about most countries around the world. To misquote Phillip Larkin, 'they **** you up, your politicians'.

So here we are, in Hungary, and the first thing we need to do is buy a *matrica* – like the Austrian vignette, it is for motorway driving. We don't think we will be going on a motorway, but it is best to have it just in case. We do not want any interactions with Hungarian police. We have had two of those in the past – one was a lot of fun, the other, more official. The fun one was back in '06, our first trip. We were in a park in Budapest with our friends and the police turned up, about twenty of them in a big van. They all ran off into the park. After about ten minutes they started trickling back to the van and were happy to have a chat with us through our interpreter, Geri. They also let the children have a look inside their van. Then Geri asked one of them to put some handcuffs on Walt, who was nine at the time, but neglected to tell Walt that it was about to happen. Good sport that he is, Walt posed for some photos looking forlorn and we all had a good laugh about it. Walt wrote about the incident in a postcard to send to school for their holiday postcard competition. 'I went to Hungary, and I got handcuffed by the police'. Of course, he won.

The not-so-fun time was on the way to Romania – we were about thirty minutes from the border when we were pulled over, along with other cars, for a full documents check. Including the MOT. It is worth having all your original documents on you because these people do *not* like photocopies. We had a similar issue with border control going into Croatia in 2019. They were not happy with the photocopy of the V5 and kept asking where the original was. As Walt pointed out, quietly, under his breath, to the occupants of the bus only, the copy looks *exactly* like the original. It was only after letting us sweat for ten minutes they let us through. The Hungarian policeman, guarding *his* side of the border, was finding it quite amusing, but that was because we were leaving *his* country. We were officially Croatia's problem at that point.

We passed the check by the Hungarian police too. We are beginning to get a little wiser every time – one year we will get it exactly right and that will be the year we don't get stopped. We even have a *matrica* for this journey, and an ice cream from the petrol station, our first interaction with the locals and it has gone well. We pay in Forints. Although Hungary is in the EU, they have not gone over to the Euro. Forints are a bit like Italian Lira used to be – you can have a million of them and you've got about two and a half grand in pounds! It makes travel more fun though when you must think a bit and do absurd calculations in your head. We are back on the road, and we keep getting beeped at. We assume it is friendly fire. There are very few GBs on the road, so we hope it is the novelty factor – we are, after all, a long way from home. Also, Olive is beautiful and commands a lot of respect, so we hope there is some bus love in those beeps.

The houses along the road are similar to the ones in Austria but maybe not quite as neat. Hungary has never had such a good economy and you can see it when you cross the border. Everything is a little shabbier; the fields are not quite so resplendent with crops; there is not so much livestock either; and the houses are functional. All have extensive land around them with a range of fencing, from white picket to forbidding chain links. Although the Russians left in the '90s, they cast a long shadow. There are few shops, and we cannot read the signs anyway, so we have no idea what they sell. The pavements are quiet too and there are no road signs so we do not even know what speed we should be doing. There is a definite sense that we have left the Europe we belong to (or did) and are now in one that we do not. We think of this area as Eastern Europe, but our friends insist it is Central Europe.

Olive is humming along though, unperturbed by any feelings of unease we may be having. Doris and the dog are asleep. They are both feeling very relaxed. It is thirty-four degrees and getting hot inside the bus. The road is smooth and though the light is still flashing, Will is happy with what the temperature gauge is telling him. Perhaps we should put a piece of tape over the flashing light. We have done that before when we had a similar issue with our 2CV. Annoying light, bit of tape, problem solved. It is like ignoring the engine management light in our more modern car or turning up the radio to cover clanking noises. For fun, I list all the things that *are* working: the windscreen can be seen out of; we have two wipers this year; one wing mirror is no longer a taped-on shower mirror; the seats can be sat on; the windows go down and back up; there is only a tiny hole in the floor that I can see the road through. The gears all work and the steering wheel steers. The brakes are okay, though you would not want to trust the handbrake on a steep hill, which is why we never leave home without Dwayne, the rock to put behind the wheels. And the horn works.

We pass an *antik* shop and a house that is *elado*. These we understand. The bric-a-brac outside the shop gives it away as an antique shop of course, and the style of the other sign is clearly a 'For Sale' sign. Somehow, seeing something so familiar and that we can understand make this seem less like a strange and distant land.

Our very first morning in Budapest in 2006, Will went for a run as he always does – wherever he is in the world he will run. It is a really good way to find out about our surroundings too as he comes back with useful information such as the location of food shops and petrol stations. On this occasion when he returned, he said to me, "This place is mad; this is major; it's like nowhere else – you cannot understand anything, not shop signs, street signs, notices in windows, nothing." He had enjoyed the experience but felt very much to be out of his depth. To not understand a word is quite scary. But it is good to get out of your comfort zone every now and then, and it is the only way we feel like real travellers! Sad to say, in ten years of visiting we still cannot read much. We know *tej* is milk; we can count to ten; and we recently learned 'left', 'right', 'straight on' and 'stop'. We know 'dog' is *kutya* and beach is *strand* so put them together and we can find the dog beach. Of course, we know 'please' and 'thank you' (we are British after all) – *kerem* and *koszonom*, but if you want to sound like you know what you are doing you say *kersie* for thanks. We know *kiraly* which means 'king' but is used for 'cool', and if you want to be really cool you say *shiraly* which means 'seagull' but is used for 'cool' due to its similarity to *kiraly*. Make sense? *Yo napot* is 'good afternoon', though we use it as 'hello'. A less formal greeting is *szia* ('sia') which means 'hi' and 'bye'. *Igen* is 'yes' and *neh* is 'no'. This is an exceedingly difficult language to learn. There are very few words that bear any resemblance to other words in any of the other European languages, with some obvious exceptions – *antik* was easy and *strand* also means beach in Dutch. Hungarian has more in common with Finnish! They also have an exceptionally long alphabet, which even a Hungarian can get lost halfway through. They do not have a word for 'he' or 'she' either which can make for some confusion when they are speaking English to you. Although perfect for this brave new world of 'they' pronouns. What is nice though is that they don't mind you trying and will let you carry on stumbling over odd words hoping to communicate. Hungarians' second language is usually German so, unlike the Dutch, they cannot segue into perfect English as soon as you start to struggle. While this is immensely helpful of the Dutch, and we do appreciate it when we are there, it does not inspire confidence or give you any chance to practise.

Hey, Walter International.

And a Tesco. Now we do feel at home. Though when you buy fish in a British Tesco it is already dead and in a plastic package, not still swimming in a tank. Apart from that, they are similar. They even have Tesco Value (blue stripey). We are passing the supermarket behemoth on a lovely smooth road, perfect for our lame bus. The ground looks scorched; they get some high temperatures here. At least one house in every village will be quite ornate with turrets and pillars, and the municipal buildings are smaller versions of what you will see in Budapest, with niches and domed roofs.

The Balcsi is another eighty kilometres; we are on a road that would take us to Croatia in the other direction. We pass many religious shrines; Catholics account for over half of the population. We pass haybale sculptures, though I am not sure what religion they represent. Maybe something more pagan? And strung everywhere are wires, electrical, telephone, on poles and pylons and through grids. It is like Beijing all over again! When wandering the alleyways of that amazing city on a brief layover between flights to Australia in 2016, we were struck by the hazardous wiring over every roof and wall and across every gap. Now when we plug in our holiday extension with several phone chargers coming from it, we refer to it as Beijing, or rather Bejing, because Will didn't realise it had that first 'i'. And obviously we have never let him forget it.

The road has gone bad now, not Romanian bad but still a lot of holes, and Olive bounces lopsidedly along on her dodgy suspension. She only seems to clank around roundabouts. The road we are on says 'no tractors, no bikes or horse-drawn vehicles', the only things on the road that are slower than us. Next year they will have added a picture of Olive. Through a shady forest it gets a little smoother, but there is now a weird whooshing sound that I try to reassure Will is due to a change in road surface. He seems to accept that and happily drives on through some tiny hamlets of half a dozen houses with no obvious signs of modern conveniences. It is not uncommon to see elderly women carrying buckets of well water back to their homes in these smaller places. It seemed bonkers to us that people could live without running water, but Bali explained that of course they did, it was just that the well water was free. These people are way smarter than us.

Time for a wee stop and a very quick ball throw for the dog but only three throws because it is too hot. We have an audience for this display of dog athleticism, a Polish family eating their lunch, some bemused chickens and a dog that looks part wolf, part donkey. It is a nice pit stop garage, with clean toilets, ample parking, picnic benches and a water tap. We feel a little guilty that we have used all this without making any purchases. To assuage our guilt Will goes to buy ice creams. He has a new concern: in the heat, Olive seems to be leaking oil because it is all splattered up the boot. This is why Will is so diligent with his liquid checks and stops every few hours to do them. This also gives Olive a break and the dog the opposite, he gets to move around, so it is the perfect travel regime. And it works. The dog is healthy; the driver is happy; and Olive always gets us there. Eventually.

There are some French and Dutch cars on the road, but it is mainly local or Austrian, Polish and German. All the drivers seem to really respect the speed limits through towns as we spend a lot of the time crawling along in slow-moving traffic. We are not entirely sure what the speed limit is because we failed to memorise the one sign we saw as we entered the country and have not seen another one since. The oil warning light is off for the first time so Will is quite relaxed and enjoying his surroundings. The churches along here have flower fairy skirt domes like upside-down tulips. Two storks are stalking in a field. It is 1.15pm and we have been on the road for four hours with two stops, but we have just got onto the M7 which leads straight to the Balcsi. It is smooth; it is empty; it is fast (for other people). Just the way Olive likes it, and as we bought the *matrica* we might as well use it. We even overtake a heavily laden plastic-wrapped Romanian van and then they overtake us back with a friendly toot. We think it was friendly, we hope it was friendly, they did not accompany it with a wave. So, it might have been a 'why did you overtake us, then slow down and force us to overtake you?' toot. But we cannot help it if the road suddenly starts to go uphill slightly, and we lose all momentum. The shrink-wrapped angry van disappears off into the distance.

New junctions are labelled in distance kilometres from Budapest so can be easily added in. *Kijarat* means 'exit' and ours is 143. It is now 1.30pm and there is a deep, dark forest next to us but at any moment we should emerge to our first view of the lake. The forest recedes and there it is, in all its sunlit shimmering beauty, the blue water surrounded by the green hills and topped with tiny white sails. A true oasis at the end of a long, long road. We are 2198 kilometres from home. We are right where we want to be. And then it disappears from view, and we use satnav (with hilarious Hungarian pronunciations) to find the actual house we will be staying in with our friends and where we will meet up with the rest of our children. Just four more kilometres to go and then at 2.06pm, with a massive backfire to announce ourselves, we have arrived.

WHY? WHY THE F*** ARE YOU GOING TO HUNGARY?

This was a question we heard frequently back in '06 when we announced our intention. Well, it all began in 2005. I was working in a redundant church in the centre of Gloucester. It was a lovely job, opening the church to visitors, April–September, three days a week. I gave guided tours, chatted with locals and tourists (redirected quite a few of them to the cathedral), sold second-hand books, organised art shows, flower festivals, children's activities and history events. There were also concerts, private bookings and links with the folk museum across the road. I spent a large part of my day sitting quietly reading, quality checking the second-hand books. I met all kinds of interesting people, some becoming good friends.

One sunny day in early July 2005, two young men came in. They were not in my usual demographic, and I was not surprised that they did not seem interested in the church but came directly to me. I looked up from my book, expecting to get a sob story of how their child was in hospital in Oxford/Bristol and they needed money to get a bus there. My standard response to this was 'well, you had better start walking then'. That may sound mean, but I know a scam when I hear one. What I got though, was a polite hello in a strong accent. At that point I would not have guessed Hungarian if my life depended on it. I did not know where Hungary was, remember?

"We are looking for some accommodation," they told me and then went on to detail their plight. They were from Hungary and had met on the plane, coming over to the UK to work. So, they had decided to team up. The job was terrible. It was to sell sets of children's encyclopaedias door to door. First of all, who buys encyclopaedias these days? In 2005, even we had got the internet at home, and we were the last on the block to do so, according to our kids. At fifteen, our eldest daughter, Maisie, had only just stopped going to the library to do her homework. Not for the books but for the internet! We have hundreds of books. Although, no children's encyclopaedias. And we still don't!

Secondly, not many people are at home during the day, so they had to start later and work into the evening. While staying at a B&B, they had nowhere else to 'be' during the day. Plus, it was an expensive option for the long term, and they intended to be in Gloucester for a few months. They had hit upon the clever idea of going round to some churches to see if a kind congregation could help them out as their Christian duty. My church was probably the only one they found to be open, and they didn't find a congregation; it had not had one of those for thirty years. But they found me.

I like to say yes to stuff. Once you get to a certain age you stop being so scared of things going wrong and you realise there is wisdom in the saying that 'you regret the things you don't do'. I like talking to people and can be quite open with complete strangers quite quickly. I once invited a nice young couple back for our regular Saturday night pizza because they were on a cycling tour of the Cotswolds and were camping nearby. We were chatting for over an hour in the church as we had so much in common, so I issued the invitation. We had a lovely evening, and we did stay in touch, mainly by text, but then they split up and neither of them wanted custody of us. In 2005 we had been a host family for three years and had had a steady stream of, mainly French, teenagers come and stay in our spare room. Usually short stays of three to five days, but we had also had some stay for two to three weeks. We had no problem sharing our home with strangers. So, I would have offered them accommodation on the spot but for the fact that we had a French girl and a Spanish girl staying for four and six weeks respectively which would take us to early August, then we would go cycling in Holland for two weeks.

However, as luck would have it, for them, only the day before I had met a friend of mine who lived just around the corner from us. Amongst other chat, she happened to mention that she had 'forgotten' to rent out the basement flat in their large eighteenth-century house for the summer, after her term-time student lets left. So, I knew where there was an empty flat. If I could not help them myself, I knew someone who could. I phoned my friend.

"Hi, Elisabeth, it's Juliet. I'm in the church and I've got two young chaps here looking for a place to stay and I was thinking about your flat…" Quietly, "They look okay, yes."

They were more than okay. They were Geri (with a hard G) and Bali (like Bolly, not the Indonesian island). These are shortened versions of their names which, apparently, is a very Hungarian thing, hence Lake Balaton becomes the Balcsi (say 'Balchi'). Geri was tall, blond and rather nice looking (it's okay, my husband agrees). Geri says himself that, unfortunately, he would have been the poster boy for the Nazis if he had been around in the 1930s. Bali was a little shorter and slight with dark hair and glasses. His fate may have been a little different in the 1930s. Their English was brilliant, their accents enchanting and they were both utterly charming. And about ten years younger than me. They still are.

Elisabeth was willing to meet with them, so I drew them a map to her house and included my name and phone number. We also agreed that if Elisabeth could have them through the summer, they could come to us when her students returned in September. So, off they went, with my map in hand, and a few hours later, I got a text: 'we love the flat – we are very happy, thank you so much'. We were having a small garden party for Will's birthday the following evening, so I told them to come. They arrived with wine and proceeded to charm four generations of Greenwood women. And one Greenwood man. Will and Geri are classic 'brothers from another mother' – they have so much in common. They like martial arts, keeping fit, knives, watches and are both funny, kind and caring. Geri has a more outrageous streak in him and can say things at times that can have you choking with laughter, most of which are unprintable. We all experienced a summer romance that year as we all, including Bali, fell in love with Geri. Bali, knowing not to even to try and compete with Geri in some things, won us over with his quiet intellect, interesting stories, curious nature and good housemateness.

During the last week of August, they moved into our spare room. Now we really got to know them and also learnt something about where they were from. I admitted to Geri that I knew very little about his homeland, of which he was enormously proud. For instance, which side were they on during the war? His response: 'the bad side'. I have since read up on that and, depending which opinion you read, it was not entirely their fault. They were rather caught between a rock and a hard place. And do not get me started on the divided opinion on Admiral Horthy! We learned that they could just about remember living under communism, that bananas had been a big issue, lack of, that is; we learned that Bali could speak six languages, that Geri was training to be a lawyer. They liked a big breakfast before going out to work the 'bookfield', as they called it, so cooked a full English every day. They were given some bikes and used them to get everywhere. Bali eventually imported his pink ladies road bike with drop handlebars back to Hungary where it was eventually stolen off a Budapest street. No one saw that coming! They came to Walter's class and did a presentation on Hungary, wowing the children with a thousand-forint note. Bali worked two extra jobs to earn more money than the 'bookfield' was providing. Geri, unsurprisingly, was quite a hit with the housewives of Gloucester and was expecting good returns from his sales. But he also got a second job, cleaning buses. We all discovered that when Geri started a sentence with, 'Jule (as he shortened my name Hungarian style, though it should be Juli) don't you mind if...' with his deep Draculaesque accent, the answer was always, 'no Geri, I don't mind at all' without needing to hear the end of that sentence. Will would regularly come home from a hard day in the classroom to find Geri cooking in *his* kitchen, wearing one of *his* T-shirts, looking very much at home, flirting with *his* wife or charming one of *his* daughters. As we were all by now a bit in love with Geri, Will 'didn't mind' either.

Then, late in September, Geri announced he was returning to Hungary. He was graduating law school and he missed his beautiful girlfriend, Nelli (short for Kornelia). Bali planned to stay on until December, so we were pleased not to be losing both in one go. Although, two friends of his were coming over to look for work so could they stay for a few days while they looked for a permanent home? "Sure," we said, "Why not?" If Bali did not mind sharing the spare room with them. In 2005 we still had all four children living at home in our five-bedroom house and luckily two of them shared a room. So, Geri got himself ready to leave and we had another party to plan, which would be happening the night before he left, though it was not a leaving party for Geri. This was also to be the night Bali's friends arrived. Nor was it a welcome party. After their long day of travelling, Bali left the party to go and meet them at the coach station and brought them back to the English family's house slap into the middle of a twenty-first birthday party. For their 2CV. And that's how we met Szilvi and Fuli, who came for three days. And stayed for three years. And that is how the Hungarians became our family.

For three years, Szilvi (don't pronounce the z) and Fuli (this is a nickname, means 'ears', given to him by his basketball coach because… that's probably obvious, he has large ears, but his real name is actually Attila) lived in our home, shared our bathroom and kitchen, cooked us some great food, cooked themselves a lot of mashed potatoes, taught us that 'did it' was 'bra' in Hungarian (it made them laugh when we said it), cleaned up after us (because I knew they would – my bad), joined in with birthdays and other celebrations, babysat our children and even came on holiday with us. We took them cycling in Holland and they loved it so much, as do we, that they returned there to live when they left us. Their first son, Levi, was born there. They met our family and we met some of theirs when they came for a visit. When the floods hit Gloucester in 2007 and we had gone to France in 'The Bus' to watch the Tour de France, our home was in a safe pair of hands with Szilvi and Fuli; the electricity was out for a short while, but there was no running water for two weeks. The resourceful Hungarians, drawing on their peasant ancestry, went down to the canal for buckets of water to use to flush the toilet with.

It was the spring of 2006, when Szilvi and Fuli had been with us for six months and Bali had been gone for three, that I looked at a map of Europe and made that pronouncement. We could drive to Hungary and see for ourselves all that we had heard about and be reunited with Geri and Bali. So, we packed all four children into Olive, or 'The Bus' as she was still known as then, waved goodbye to Szilvi and Fuli at our house and set off for their homeland. They would fly out later and see us there.

Fuli had drawn us a map. We were to drive into Budapest and, on a certain day at a certain time, Bali would be waiting by a very distinctive derelict factory building with an advert on the side (I forget what for) and a large clock tower attached. Fuli drew all this. How James Bond does that sound? Meeting our Hungarian contact under a clock tower in Budapest. So, we drove across Europe, had hot pain au chocolat for breakfast in Belgium, had our first encounter with the police in Germany, stayed with Gwynn and Elke and met toddler Alex, saw Vienna, had to show our passports to get into Hungary for the first and only time. Then we followed the main road into Budapest, the M1, as the map dictated. Saw the clock tower, looking exactly like Fuli's drawing, and there was Bali. He was sitting on the kerb at the edge of the parking area, not looking too much like he had been there for a while. It was a highly successful meet-up, thank goodness for mobile phones, but still, when you are in a rusty old bus, anything can happen! It worked again in 2013, only that time Bali was not sitting on the kerbside but in his own BMW. We were still in the same rusty old bus. We looked out for the building when we drove into Budapest the next time, in 2019, but sadly, it has now been demolished. That is a little piece of our shared history gone for good.

Bali hopped into the bus and guided us through his city to his home. This was an apartment in a big block of flats built in a square with a courtyard and water tower in the centre. We parked the bus outside on the street. Huge doors led into a cool entranceway with wide stone steps leading off it. At the second floor we exited onto a balcony and walked past the front doors of two flats to reach Bali's in the corner. His elderly neighbours had lived there since the war and took a daily constitutional along the balcony and back. They seemed to appreciate our cheery *yo napot* whenever we saw them. Bali had two rooms connected by a short hallway which the bathroom was off, opposite the front door. Turn right for the kitchen; turn left for the living room with mezzanine sleeping platform amply spaced under the high ceilings. Tall windows looked out onto the inner courtyard. In the kitchen, a large pot of chicken paprikash waited for us, cooked by Bali's mum. She had also made him go out and buy extra plates, glasses, cutlery and placemats for his six house guests. This was our first taste of real Hungary, and we loved it. The food was delicious and being in a real Hungarian home with real Hungarian neighbours (none of the fake kind) was thrilling. We slept on camping mattresses and mats under Bali's platform bed. Maisie opted for a little more privacy by sleeping in the kitchen. It was hard to sleep though because it was so hot. Despite the high ceilings and the open windows, not a whiff of a breeze circulated, and Bali had no air conditioning. You didn't even want to lie down because that was too much contact for your sweaty back.

We loved our stay there, right in the heart of Buda (Pest is on the other bank; they became one in 1873), a short tram ride from the sights. We went everywhere by tram, leaving the bus to stay parked at Bali's flat in a leafy side street. Car ownership was rare under communism, so the public transport system had to make up for it. So frequent and so cheap you could hop on and off rather than bother walking to the corner shop. We just followed

Bali like a line of ducklings and did what he did; I'm not sure if we always paid.

Bali was an excellent guide; he is proud of his city, and we could see it was a city to be proud of. The history is reflected in the architecture as different invaders left their mark. We explored the tourist Budapest but also some one-off shops and cafes that only a local can find. We saw Heroes Square, the Grand Market, the Parliament buildings and the Church of St Stephen. We spent a whole day at the large thermal baths and had a lovely afternoon on Margrits Island. We met up with Geri in the park where Walter got handcuffed by the police (that was all Geri's doing). He was living in his university town of Pecs but had family in Budapest. We enjoyed another meal of chicken paprikash at their house with huge watermelon smiles for dessert.

After four days in Budapest, we all piled into the bus (she seats eight, all with seatbelts) and drove out to the Balcsi. It was almost an uneventful journey of 155 kilometres to get to Revfulop where Geri's grandparents had a holiday home until we were very nearly there. We heard a large petrol mower start up as we passed through one of the towns that line the shores of the lake. As we drove away it seemed to be following us, except it was not a petrol mower, it was the bus. We pulled over; Will got underneath to discover that she had spat out a spark plug. Bali's parents happened to be holidaying nearby, so they came over to offer assistance, which gave us the opportunity to thank his mum for that first night's meal and having plates to eat off. They then accompanied us the few miles left as we limped on to the grandparents' house. A royal welcome awaited us in the form of Mommy and Poppy, Geri's grandparents and owners of the home we were to stay in for the next week. Another meal of chicken paprikash had been prepared for all, including Bali's parents. Our Hungarian friends were worried that we thought there was only one dish Hungarians could cook but it was, to us, an obvious choice as an introduction to Hungarian cookery, not as heavy as goulash, full of traditional paprika and peppers and absolutely delicious. This version was made noteworthy in that it was served to us by Mommy (a sweet little lady in her late seventies) in a bikini. She then changed into a more formal one piece to go for an evening swim before they returned to their first home in nearby Tapolca, just nineteen kilometres away.

Neither Mommy or Poppy or Bali's parents spoke English (why should they?) so communication was through Geri and Bali and mime. They found our attempts at Hungarian highly amusing and encouraged our *kerems* and *kersies*. We spent some more time with Mommy and Poppy on that trip and on subsequent ones until they sadly passed away in 2014, one not surviving the other by very long. Unfortunately, our Hungarian never improved enough to really talk to them much, but Will once spent an enjoyable evening with Poppy communicating solely through the mediums of drawing and mime. Poppy made up his own sign for Maisie (an avid reader), which was the 'book' sign from charades. On the visits when she was not with us, he would make that sign and we knew it meant that he remembered her and was wondering where she was.

That first trip though, after the 'grown-ups' had had their swim and left, Mommy and Bali's mum chatting away like lifelong friends even though they had only just met, we were left in their little house to be our home for the rest of our stay in Hungary.

Second home ownership is very normal in Hungary, possibly because for so long they could not travel abroad. They bought their second homes near the lakes or spas and then handed them down through the generations. This is something we aspire to in the West and yet, here in Hungary, it seemed as if everyone had one. We also give holidaying at home a fancy name, a 'staycation' but out there, for generations, it was just what you did. Poppy had built this house himself on a plot of land big enough for a house, many fruit trees and vines, outdoor dining, an outdoor shower and a firepit plus parking for two cars. The house was up some steps to a small veranda; under the house were cellars and a workshop area. There was a communal living/dining area, a tiny kitchen and a shower room downstairs plus two large sitting rooms/bedrooms that could sleep four to six people. Geri took one of these, Bali the other. Upstairs was all for us, another bathroom, a small double for Will and me and, at the front with a view of the lake, a beautiful big room with three single beds and room for Doris's airbed/sleeping bag combi. When Szilvi and Fuli also arrived, they were able to share the large settee bed in the dining area, though six-feet-plus Fuli had to have his feet out onto a chair.

Outside amongst the fruit trees was a long table with two long benches and a firepit. Hungarians don't really barbecue like we do. Instead, they have a lined hole in the ground to build a fire in and then they suspend a pot from a tripod over it and cook up huge pots of goulash, fish stew and, of course, chicken paprikash. Food is often one of the lasting memories of a good holiday and our favourite image from that stay is all of us around that long table, in the warmth of the dying sun, amidst the whirr of the crickets, eating goulash from a bowl with bread as a spoon.

Lake Balaton serves as the Hungarian seaside. Most of the best bits of beach require a small payment to access them. There is a big rivalry between the north side of the lake and the south side. Geri is an ardent 'northsider', having been brought up on that side in nearby Tapolca (say it like this: 'tap-o-wetsa') and of course, holidaying in Révfülöp as a child. He says that the only good thing about the south side is the view of the north side. We only knew the north at first because we stayed in Révfülöp each time we went. From there we drove out to the local vineyards and sampled the wine; we visited the beautiful town of Badacsony and we went to the Valley of the Arts festival in the villages of Kapolcs, Taliándörögd and Vigántpetend which, for ten days in August, becomes a huge art venue, every house displaying artistic creations for sale and booths selling food on every street, plus music and performance. We drove to Tihany where you can catch the ferry across to the south and from there we drove down to Pecs, Geri's university town, 155 kilometres away. Here we met Nelli, his beautiful girlfriend, also a student at Pecs University. As we were *all* a little in love with Geri, it would have been very easy to be jealous of Nelli, but she wins your heart too. They are a power couple! Nelli is one of the kindest people you could hope to meet, always looking to help you out or do something nice. In the first moments of meeting her she went off to buy us some postcards and she has continued to bring us gifts ever since. She has loved meeting our children and seeing them become adults, complimenting our parenting skills and the family we have created. Nelli goes out of her way to make you feel good about yourself, a rare quality. We all absolutely adore her.

When Geri and Nelli got married, we flew over for the wedding, there was no time to drive, and two of our daughters were part of the bridal party. Meredith was to be a bridesmaid, something Nelli had decided on the first time she met her. When I also casually mentioned to Geri that nine-year-old Doris was upset not to be involved, he said, "Jule, I will fix this." And he did. If we bought her a little white dress she could join in as a flower girl. Luckily, Maisie and Walt were happy to just be guests! We didn't want to take over. It was a very overwhelming occasion, we felt privileged to be a part of it, and it is the wedding we hold all other weddings accountable to. No expense was spared for the guests to feel valued. And this is how it should be. When I told Geri's aunt that at English weddings there is usually a paying bar, she looked at me like I had said guests were served bread and water only. On arrival at the reception venue after two ceremonies, one religious, one legal, Doris was asked what she wanted to drink, and she asked for a cup of tea. The bride herself translated the request to the staff, "A cup of tea for the English girl. With milk!" and 'the English girl' got her beverage of choice. The rest of us had unlimited cocktails which necessitated getting two each time because the queue was so long, or you could stay in your seat and wait for a waiter to bring a tray of random drinks and choose what you wanted. The food was delicious, of course – there was a table of cakes and at midnight more hot food was brought out. We took part in a traditional wedding dance which allows the new couple to be given a lot of money in a fun way. The bride and groom dance while the guests throw money at them, or cheques in those days. Unfortunately, Nelli had a knee problem so was unable to fulfil her dancing duties. She sat on a chair banging the pan for the money with a spoon while Geri did the dancing for the two of them. Which is how every good marriage should begin. Apparently, the guests give more money based on how good the hospitality of the wedding was, though Bali may have been pulling our legs on that one. While other guests wrote out their cheques, Bali was very cool and just danced up to Nelli and flicked a note into her pan. No one had told us about this tradition, so we had bought them an actual present, some pillowcases. Very English. At midnight, the bride and groom changed out of their wedding clothes into party outfits to signify that they were now husband and wife not a bride, not a groom. They must stay until the last guests leave because they are the hosts. We partied until 3.00am when someone noticed that Doris was asleep on the table. Geri and Nelli were there until 6.00am.

We spent the night in the tiny holiday home of Nelli's grandma where Walt famously got to sleep with the ants on the floor. We ate cake from the selection at the wedding for breakfast and spent the day recovering from our night of excess at the spa baths across the street from our little house. We had wondered why Nelli's grandma had a holiday home in such an odd little place, nowhere near the Balcsi, but on discovering that spa we understood. It was an outdoor series of pools of varying temperatures, sparsely populated and costing about two or three pounds each to gain entry. This was to be by far the best way to recover from our heavy night of food, drink and merriment. I highly recommend it. We then spent the evening at Nelli's childhood home with the newly-weds, her family and our friends. Geri and Nelli would not go on honeymoon until later and had spent their 'wedding night' under her mum's roof. Geri was sporting a T-shirt with a bride and groom on it and the words 'Game Over' written underneath them. Only Geri can get away with this kind of thing. When we drove away that night Meredith said what we were all thinking, "I'm so glad you worked in that church, Mum," and for the millionth time we all were thankful that the stars had aligned to send those two Hungarian chaps into that church on the day after I had spoken to Elisabeth about her empty flat. From such humdrum moments, great things can happen.

Before we left the wedding, with Geri's cousin who lives in England as interpreter, I managed to convey to a slightly bewildered mother of the bride my extreme gratitude for my family being part of her daughter's wedding. When little Nelli and her mum dreamed of her wedding day they may have known the groom would be handsome, she may have drawn pictures of her bridesmaids' dresses and one of those bridesmaids may have had red hair, but they cannot have envisaged two English girls being part of it. I love that about life. I hope, through my interpreter, I got that point

Day Five

across. That we were absolutely thrilled to be there. In 2016 Geri, Nelli, Szilvi and Fuli came over for Maisie's wedding to Adam and gave it their Hungarian seal of approval. Fuli got everyone drunk on Pálinka.

Now they all have babies themselves and we are happy 'aunts' and 'uncles' to Hanna and Szofie, to Levi and Samu and to Bence and Lila (her birth was the reason Bali and Aniko could not make Maisie's wedding!). We are their English family.

In 2017, we have just arrived at the house on the south side of the lake. Poppy and Mommy's house belongs to another family member now and is not available for our use. Szilvi and Fuli have found a large house in Balatonboglár. It is a little further from the beach but, wow, what a beach! The south side is famous for its shallow, sandy access. You can walk out for one hundred metres and still the water is barely to your waist. On the north side, it is chest high a few feet from shore. The shore is grassy and there are trees for shade. Shops sell beach equipment, cheap beer, *langos* and *palascinta*. This is what we come for. To lie in the shade, play in the water and eat and drink. We will go out for a meal that is so ridiculously cheap, even with wine included, that twenty-year-old Walt will offer to pay for all. A generous gesture from one so young, but it will only set him back sixty pounds. We play word games in the evening; their English is good enough for them to participate fully though Fuli does get a bit stuck describing what bears do in the woods, and Will, the native English speaker, starts describing a diary when the word was dairy (I have mentioned his poor reading skills haven't I?). Geri and Nelli join us for two nights and Bali and Aniko for one. We are all together again. Aniko is shy about her English until she hears about Will's dairy/diary mix-up, then she feels more confident. We all watch a fantastic thunderstorm from our house balcony, shrieking when lightning seems to hit the house opposite, only to find out the next day that it hit a tree in the garden of the house next door to the house opposite. Which is close enough! We ride the summer bobsleigh, eat watermelon bought from roadside vendors; we take the dog to the dog beach; and we shop in Tesco. Hot nights are thick with mosquitos, crickets and other strange sounds, and dogs pierce our slumber with their barking. Our dog barely responds. We eat red pepper and home-made salamis for breakfast, cook goulash over the firepit, heat up lard on a stick like we do marshmallows, to drip it onto bread with sausages. The wine is cheap, the company is rich. These are good times. It started in a church in Gloucester and now we drive across half a continent to continue it. It is worth every kilometre and every clanking, leaking, light flashing, buzzing, police-avoiding, back-aching, oil-checking, incomprehensible, overheated moment.

Under a Belgian Flyover

If it all started in a redundant church in Gloucester in 2005, it nearly all ended under a flyover in Belgium in 2013. All six Greenwoods were in the bus because it was the year Maisie and Meredith flew to Budapest and joined us for the Balcsi part of the holiday and the trip home. This return journey was to include a slight detour to Maastricht to see Szilvi and Fuli and brand-new baby Levi. We had stayed over at Gwynn and Elke's on the way back which we don't often do but it was a nice opportunity for them to see the whole family. The first incident of that fateful return journey happened soon after leaving their home. We were pulling up a hill in heavy traffic on the motorway heading away from Vienna. Without any prelude, every warning light and buzzer went off at once and the temperature gauge needle shot so far off the scale it was not seen again for days.

"I've got nothing!" Will exclaimed, meaning he had no power, and nothing was doing what it was supposed to be doing. He pulled over immediately onto the narrow hard shoulder and jumped out in time to witness a puddle of coolant forming underneath us. He needed to see what was going on in the engine and the only way to get to it was to remove all the luggage. Rather than pile it at the roadside where lorries were hurtling past us, Will started to pass it through to the kids in the back. Some of it was passed to me in the front as it piled up around us, essentially trapping us inside the bus. Will was on his own at the back, head in the engine. Grim silence reigned as we sat and listened to his exclamations. Walt, who happened to be sitting closest to the boot for once, tried to interpret the sounds and signs as Will assessed the situation. It was the alternator. And it wasn't where it should be. One of the bolts holding it in place had sheared off so the alternator was hanging from its bracket. The solution was to use a bolt from the sliding door (rendering that immobile and necessitating entry and exit through the boot from that point on), wrapping it in the trusty green garden wire and chocking it with a match. It was a classic Boy Scout/Heath Robinson repair and it worked. We shifted all the luggage back into the boot and continued driving. We drove for a further two hours and then found a campsite near Grein. We slept four in the bus and two in a tent that night.

The following day we crossed into Germany and a new/old issue reared its menacing little head. The familiar metallic clanking from the wheels indicated a problem with the bearings as experienced in France in 2012 when we had what turned out to be the Best Breakdown Ever. Could this one go so well? Could we be that lucky twice? The mood in the bus was low that day – no one was speaking; everyone was listening. Or asleep. Kids are remarkably resilient to this kind of stress. Partly because they trust their dad to deal with whatever arises and partly because he worries enough for everyone. They recently found a wooden plaque with 'If Dad can't fix it, we're screwed' on it and that now hangs in Olive behind his head.

I watched Will's face which was tense with stress. We managed to drive all day but could not cope with a foray off the motorway to find a campsite, so we just holed up at a services. There are always going to be lorry drivers sleeping in their cabs at services, and you do get the occasional campervan joining them, so it is a bit like a campsite. We parked up opposite the toilet block, so we had facilities and running water. There were picnic benches to eat our supper at, cooked on our portable stove. There was no possibility or inclination to set up the tent though, so we all six must sleep in the bus. We could fit. Three of us on the 'bed', one on the 'mezzanine' and the two shortest members of the family slept across the bus widthways. Eleven-year-old Doris was across the front seats with some luggage filling the gap between the seats. This had been her usual spot for many years by this point, on a blow-up bed with sleeping bag attached. She couldn't fit in the sleeping bag bit of it anymore, but the airbed still served a purpose. Nineteen-year-old Meredith, but luckily less-than-five-feet-tall Meredith, was in the boot, also lying on luggage but with some blankets for cushioning. Since the side door wouldn't open, we would have to climb over one of them to get out if anyone needed to pee in the night. I think the word we are looking for here is 'cosy'. Sardines comes to mind too. At least it kept us warm in the night, and luckily everyone has strong bladders.

Breakfast was a sombre occasion, but we made the decision to keep going to Maastricht. Maybe we could use the local know-how of Szilvi and Fuli to find a mechanic to fix the problem as smoothly as they had in France. We would have somewhere nice to stay while it was being done and we could pay for it on our credit card (though this was the trip where we could not remember our pin). The only time constraint was our booked tunnel crossing, though previous experience had taught us that these were very flexible. Maisie had to be at work in three days', but if you are not in the country, you are not in the country. What is a boss going to do about that? We would worry about that in two and a half days' time. So, we left our parking area/campsite at 9.40am and set off in the direction of Holland, stopping *every* thirty minutes to check the liquids. Coolant was haemorrhaging from somewhere; Will suspected a crack in the engine itself. It seemed like this could actually be the end of our beloved bus. We might have to decide whether to spend a lot of money on her or give her up. At this point in the journey there was some levity (for the passengers) from the interaction with the German police that led to the driver's aborted pee-in-the-cup situation.

On the road again after that, the wheels kept turning, eating up the kilometres to Maastricht (thank goodness they don't live in Groningen in the north). It was 4.00pm, satnav was saying we were an hour away but many, many stops later (every half an hour, remember?), we arrived at 6.45pm. It was a triumphant arrival. We met Levi, breathed in his new baby smell; we ate; we slept; we buried our heads in the sand. The next morning, we were refreshed and hopeful, plus we had a newborn baby to cuddle some more. Will had some theories. He and Fuli had both stood looking at the bus, scratched their heads for a bit, crawled underneath it and started the engine. Will thought the problem was with the rear right-hand wheel. He thought the coolant and oil issues had stabilised and were not the main problem, though this may well have been relative. He completely rejected staying for an extra day to seek assistance from a real mechanic. He was confident we would get home and get Maisie to work on time.

"Are you sure?"

"Yes. We'll get home."

Okaaay. So, after a quick, but necessary, shopping trip to Hema, our favourite shop in Holland, if not the world, we said our goodbyes to Szilvi, Fuli and Levi. We then loaded up, including a bike rack on the back for a couple of Dutch bikes we are importing, just to add some more strain on the poor old bus, and we hit the road at midday. We must be back on English soil tonight so Maisie could be at work in the morning. No pressure. We trundled off and it was not long before we were in Belgium. The problem with Belgium, and please do not take offence here any Belgian readers because I have clarified this with some real Belgians and they *agree*, but the problem with Belgium is the traffic. And the problem with an aged vehicle is that if she is moving slowly in traffic, she gets hot, and the clanking gets worse. So, at all costs we must avoid traffic. In our vast experience (two separate journeys), the worst traffic is on the ring roads around the city centres. Therefore, it would be advisable to avoid any big cities, Brussels especially. We had driven around Brussels twice before, at different times of the day, neither could be considered 'rush hour', but we had ended up stuck in the most appalling amount of slow-moving traffic we had ever seen. Right now, in our hot and angry bus, this would essentially be the death of her. So, we tried, we really tried to avoid Brussels, and we nearly did, despite satnav's insistence, but instead we got stuck around Antwerp. We were crawling along; it was getting hotter and hotter; the buzzer was going crazy; the brakes were sticking; and the wheel sounded like it was going to fall off.

There was no other solution than that we had to get out of this queue, stop moving and let things cool off. We found an exit and drove down and round a ramp to come to rest on some wasteland underneath the road we were just on. Will turned off the engine and slumped his head onto the steering wheel. We sat in silence. The minutes ticked by. To be completely honest, I was silently seething. I said we should have stayed in Holland with Szilvi and Fuli and got things fixed there, whatever the expense. What on earth did we do if she wouldn't move now? We were so stuck; we could not have been more stuck. We could not call anyone. There was no AA help for us. We had driven ourselves into a hole.

This moment would go down in our family folklore as the 'worst of times', that moment of darkness and despair under a Belgian flyover. It was the perfect spot for such gloom, a neglected area of nothingness between the motorway and an industrial estate, strewn with litter amongst gigantic, graffitied concrete pillars supporting the motorway. It was the very definition of bleak. We weren't even under the sky; if we looked up, all we could see was concrete. This could not be her final resting place. It just couldn't. Not after all the joy she had brought to us.

"Let's just set fire to it," came a helpful suggestion from the back. No sentimentality whatsoever from that quarter.

"We should have got a train." And another.

"Seriously guys, do I need to call work and say I won't be in tomorrow?" Maisie asked.

Will lifted his head from the steering wheel. His hand went to the keys still dangling from the ignition. The keys that had a keyring attached for all the places this bus had taken us in ten years. Paris, Copenhagen, Barcelona, France, Holland and Hungary. And not just once but many times, so many wonderful trips.

"No. We'll get home." He turned the keys, and the engine started. Immediately, the mood lifted. No one expected that to happen. We were all behind her now, willing her on. The family was united; we were as one. We clanked our way back onto the road and back to the curving ramp that would get us up to the motorway. As we gathered speed up the ramp, the clanking did indeed die away, and we were smiling and chattering again. It was going to be alright! Maisie put away her phone; she didn't need to call work. Instead, she started to play some music. The deep, gravelly voice of Johnny Cash accompanied our flight and the atmosphere changed instantly to euphoria, or hysteria, it was hard to tell. Johnny drowned out any sounds from underneath us. This was amazing. Will thumped the centre of the steering wheel in an encouraging gesture.

"Come on, bus, you can do it," and to the rest of us, "As long as the traffic is moving, we'll be okay." The windows were open, so the wind whipped away his words and the noise from within increased. We were nearly there; the ramp was flattening out at the top in readiness to join the motorway. We looked eagerly ahead, praying to the traffic gods for fast-moving cars to come into view. "As long as the traffic is moving…"

It was not. They were going so slowly we barely had to merge in. It was more like parking. This was our worst possible scenario for how this drama was going to play out. The chatter died; Johnny Cash was silenced as gloom descends once more. For an all-too-brief moment, we had sniffed the sweet scent of triumph. But then, a sign! Not from the traffic gods – they had deserted us, the bastards – but an ordinary motorway sign with destinations on it. We were in the wrong lane! The other lane was flowing freely and that was the lane we needed to be in. We literally cheered. Until reality struck. How to join a fast-moving line of traffic from a dead halt in a dying bus with a clanking back wheel and an acceleration rate of zero to forty-five kilometres per hour in about twenty minutes? With a driver on the wrong side to see the gaps. This was not going to be easy. There was only one solution. He was going to have to trust his family. As one, Maisie and I, who were both sitting on the left side with an accessible window, stuck our heads out and screamed, "Goooooo, now, now, now," at the appropriate moment.

We made it. Not just out of our lane but into the fast lane and down the road at a solid eighty-eight kilometres per hour, not a clank to be heard. At 7.00pm we were just sixty kilometres from Calais and we were full of optimism. Every wheel turn got us closer, closer to everything we held dear, our homes and loved ones, our valid AA membership.

Before we knew it, we were in France for the last bit and then, the holy grail of Calais McDonald's. Every road trip has ended here. We thought we were not going to make it this time and that made the burgers taste especially great. Try it, it is the best way to enjoy a McDonald's. We went crazy and spent fifty euros. We have a photo of that moment – it is going dark; the camera is at a weird angle, but we are sitting on deckchairs in the Eurotunnel car park, waving burgers at the camera, grinning like maniacs. It had taken us eight hours to get there. The AA route planner calculates this route from Maastricht to Calais, for an average car, at three hours and eleven minutes. The average car does not have a top speed of eighty-eight kilometres per hour and does not have to stop for oil, coolant and other liquid checks every thirty minutes (he sets a timer on his watch for them). The average car could not snatch itself back from an abyss of despair under a Belgian flyover. The average car does not fit the six Greenwoods. But who wants to be average?

The passport guy validated us, asking us how far we had come. "Hungary," we told him, and that he had no idea how glad we were to see him. He was impressed. We dared them to search us if they wanted; we didn't care. We were here.

And that is the end. The rest was easy. We got on a train. Went through the tunnel under the sea. We dropped Maisie off in Stamford Hill at midnight. She got to work on time the next day. We drove on to Gloucester, arriving at 3.00am. We got home. Just as Will said we would.

This book is printed on paper from sustainable sources managed under the Forest Stewardship Council (FSC) scheme.

It has been printed in the UK to reduce transportation miles and their impact upon the environment.

For every new title that Matador publishes, we plant a tree to offset CO_2, partnering with the More Trees scheme.

MORE TREES
LET'S PLANT A BILLION TREES

For more about how Matador offsets its environmental impact, see www.troubador.co.uk/about/